The Journey of Ardra Knight

The Journey of Ardeo Knight

A Cap & Gown Mystery

By

William A. C. Polk

Library of Congress Control Number:		2006906199
ISBN 10:	Hardcover	1-4257-2466-3
	Softcover	1-4257-2465-5
ISBN 13:	Hardcover	978-1-4257-2466-5
	Softcover	978-1-4257-2465-8

This book was printed in the United States of America.

To order additional copies of this book, contact:
Xlibris Corporation
1-888-795-4274
www.Xlibris.com
Orders@Xlibris.com

34623

TABLE OF CONTENTS

DEDICATION

A prayer

for:

Every person that is likely to have a role in the—

Physical

Social

Emotional

Educational

Moral/ethical

Development of a black male.

for:

Every person responsible for their

Security

Protection

Nurturance

Love

Support

Guidance.

So that:

Every child will become a

Successful,

Achieving,

Contributing

Self-actuating and happy

Member of society.

ACKNOWLEDGEMENTS

I acknowledge with sincere appreciation my many friends, family and co-workers who gave me commendable assistance with putting this document into its final form. Especially, Patricia Woolard, the Media Design specialist at my place of employment, who helped finalize the cover design. The assistance of all these folks has been invaluable.

Other coworkers and friends listened to, and read some of my ideas, and were exceedingly helpful in clarifying and strengthening them.

My gratitude to all is boundless.

PROLOGUE

* * *

Rudell, one of my 9th grade boys, had been shot just the night before in what was commonly called "a rumble" in the street. I had just come back to my office from the hospital where I visited with his distraught mother, along with an "uncle" and two other teenagers. All were with him in the room. He was unconscious, and didn't even know that anybody was there. I was just about to leave, when his mother, with a heart wrenching, tormented cry, wailed something like, "Ooh Lord, he's gonna die, I know it! He's not gonna grow up!"

Somehow, in an uncanny way, I knew that her cry was a fact—the truth.

And it ripped through me like a chainsaw. On my way out of the room I banged through the door so hard it put a dent in the wall.

"Damn," I swore to myself. "When is it going to end? We've got to face this, time and again, and it tears my heart out. I'm ready to quit right now!"

I left the hospital desperately searching for answers. All I could think about as I walked toward the parking lot was the young boys I work with in school; all the crap many of them have endured and tangled with, and all the people hurt as a result of it. I got so upset I wanted to cry. And I almost did cry, feeling nearly as sorry for myself as for that kid and his mother. I was feeling hopeless and helpless. And with a long anguished sigh, I moaned in a silent rage, "I'm an old man, and I've waited so long to see the young men of my future do better than I did. I know I can't fix the roadblocks that always stand in their way, by myself. But help is hard to find."

Everybody's saying, "This ought to be done, or that ought to be done." But when a bomb is about ready to explode in our faces, that particular bomb gets defused. Everybody then gets back to doing whatever's been done before—exactly nothing. Meanwhile, thousands of other bombs are still ticking!

By this time you know what I'm ranting about, It's all about my young cohorts, who, like Rudell—for reasons they don't understand—can't come off their street corner mentality, or who won't, or can't succeed in school. I know they want to.

Many times—I've heard them say things like:

"Man, I wish I could stop runnin' and catch up with livin'."

"Everybody' else's got what they want, but I can't get it."

"My little hustle is scary. I'm sicka' duckin' cops. I'm sicka' lyin' to my Momma, and I'm sure sicka' them damn teachers who make me feel so pitiful and no good."

Young Black males, like Rudell exist all over this country. Every story is different, but thank God, they all don't end in tragic death. Although many escape death, and even have successful lives, many others have experiences that are, in some ways, worse than death.

Consider the reality that tens-of-thousands of brilliant young black men are underachieving in life, and have quit school. Consequently, they must wrestle ill equipped for survival and recognition. Forgotten and discarded, they help feed the insatiable appetites of jails, prison systems and funeral homes across the country.

This fictional story is about Ardro Knight, just one of these young black males. Throughout Ardro's story he encounters mysterious social controls that that are hostile to the well being of every black male. Ardro—first subdued by—then endured, learned, tangled with, and finally conquered these forces that were hindering his progress toward putting, at least a High School cap and gown on his sturdy young body.

Paradoxically, he encountered forces in his journey that many successful blacks did not even want to discuss. For varied historical reasons, many who do achieve success will not admit to, or talk constructively about outstripping their peers. First of all, no one likes to talk about those things that separate him from his peer group; it makes him uncomfortable. Secondly, many middle class blacks deem it demeaning to the image of the black race to talk about the fallen—detracting from those who do succeed. For many, racial pride is injured by discussions of perceived shortcomings, as opposed to recognized strengths.

Even now, internal emotional forces are just as potent as external social, ones. For instance: Success for many young black males adds an uncalled-for burden to their life. For them, it is totally unacceptable be recognized by their peers as different, (smart—Studious). Many are unwilling, or unable, to bear up under this kind of success. It is almost unbearable to be different from, and to resist the pressures of peers; sometimes his family, and other community role groups.

Success in the real world, such as that achieved by Ardro in this story, is fully possible. However, success is regrettably an entirely different thing in neighborhood and school peer groups. Most young black men choose success in their peer group. It's family.

Remarkably, in spite of these forces, thousands can and do achieve success. It is however, too often at the expense of the unembellished abandonment of many thousands more who fade into the tumultuous fabric of their environment until—suddenly, their pictures appear—in the newspaper or on TV—indicating that they are facing a terrible fate.

Ironically, many individuals who are uncomfortable with these ideas and fear injury to racial pride can be pivotal, if inspired, to help create the potency and the capability to change the future for young black males. It is essential however, to recognize that none can do it alone.

Furthermore, support from everyone, can be invaluable in helping all black males overcome historically imposed internal forces that cause success—anxiety—the fear of ostracism by friends and loved ones.

The purpose of Ardro's story is therefore, to explore the factors that cause so many young black males to choose defeating behaviors The story also explores social and cultural environments, in which significant groups, "Role Groups," play roles in the development of every individual.

We will meet Ardro's family, his School, his Teachers, his Peers, his Church, the Community service Agencies, Law Enforcement, Health facilities, etc.—all having the responsibility for providing and satisfying, on a daily basis, his social, emotional, developmental, security, moral guidance, and companionship needs.

It is important to note here, that—although this story is fiction, and the characters are fictional—every reader will probably be able to find him or her self in one of the characters.

This story gives you a chance to look at the functions of each "Role Group" in our communities. These have created—and still create—the fabric of the prime factors relevant to the Cap and Gown mystery. It is intended that by the end of my story each reader will have considered alternative thoughts, perceptions and deeds. This consideration will enhance the chances that these vital Role Groups will assure that every student, including black males, achieves what he is capable of achieving.

* * *

I

Ardro
The Beginning

Brody Browne was sitting at his desk, just scribbling. His scribbles made no sense to me, and I don't think they even made sense to him. "Just passin' time" He piteously said, as I dashed into his office.

I was mad! I had just caught a glimpse of three boys being hauled away by Juvenile authorities. Didn't know what happened. I wasn't called to do anything.

"What happened?" I hollered. What's going on with those kids?

He just kept scribbling. As I sat down uninvited, right in front of his desk, I could tell that he was about to do an "unmanly" thing—cry. And he welcomed my intrusion.

"Well, what happened?" I asked again.

Anger began to replace the tears. Feverishly, He broke into a tirade about kids 'having no home upbringing', about parents or non-parents shoving their kids off to school, just to get them out of their hair for a few hours. He was seething, as he then haltingly told me that those three boys I saw being hauled away had molested a 9th grade girl in the stairwell. And then, when caught by two passing teachers, pushed both of them down the steps—giving one a severe back injury and the other a sprained ankle.

I was stunned. The teacher with the sprained ankle was a close friend. She and I had worked together, and succeeded in keeping a kid from dropping out. Now that kid was in the juvenile van, on his way to jail. Things had happened so fast that Brody, the principal, never thought about calling me during what came to be called "the attack".

I'm looking at Brody now—still nervously scribbling, and on the inside, fervently looking for answers.

"Ya' kinda' late Bill" He said weakly, "but I'm sure glad you came in.

"Why?

"Well, I want to call their moms, but . . . ."

"But what?"

"You know!"

Deep down inside I did know, and I hated it. "Yeah, I know." I grunted.

The kid who pushed Cecile Bundy, my teacher friend, was Ardro—Ardro Knight. Many times have I talked with Ardro's Mom, Helene. Each time she'd show up, she'd be different. At first, she wouldn't admit that Ardro was unruly at home. Later, she swore up and down that her only child was "good as gold," sweet to her. Next time, she was so mad with him that she wanted to beat the stew out of him and kick him out of the house. At other times, she was awash in tears.

"He's too much responsibility," she'd declare. "He wants things I can't buy for him."

She fumed, "I can't stand it anymore."

One time, in her frustration and helplessness, she said she hated him. But the last time I saw her, she was scared to death that Ardro would be taken away from her, or would be in jail for life.

As I sat with Brody, I could almost hear his dread. He seemed to be in a dull stupor. What was he going to say to her this time? And how was he going to handle her outbursts?

As we sat there—he in his stupor, and I in my reverie—we remembered the many times before, listening to her tedious tirades, even without such a crisis. We wondered, "What does this woman want?—REALLY need?" Was she feeling unloved? Ardro loved her. He told me so. But she never really knew it. Everybody needs love.

"Does anybody else love her?" I mused. If so, was Ardro getting in the way of that love?

I realized that she clearly couldn't control Ardro. She didn't know how. That was one of her biggest complaints. He, along with the rest of her life, was controlling her. She, at times, was afraid of him, and she certainly feared for him. Fear was a big part of her existence.

The only place she really felt safe was at St John's, the big church just down the street from her. There, she'd get out her repressed feelings and refresh her spirit by singing and shouting. But even there, in the crowded church, she'd be alone in her catharsis. Everybody else there would be doing the same thing.

"Humnn!" Brody's sigh broke into my pondering.

Watching his anxiety, and sharing it, as this stuff kept running through my mind, I wondered what Helene's miseries had to do with Ardro's kissing that screaming girl, and then pushing his favorite teacher down the steps. I wondered how he must be feeling now—probably as helpless as his Momma.

Counselors, I thought, catch hell trying to figure out what to say kids—parents—teachers in situations like this. I knew the probable consequences Ardro faced. Brody had just explained to me that Michael, one of Ardro's partners in "The attack," had his hand down inside the girl's jeans. We all knew he was going to be expelled. But Ardro—if he was lucky—would have a JV hearing and be suspended for the rest of the semester. Now, I knew, that for him, it would be just like being expelled. I knew he'd drop out.

No ifs, ands or buts about it—he'd drop out! What could I do for him? What could I do for Helene? Exactly nothing

Time and time again, I've run into such dilemmas. The names are different but the outcomes, too often, are the same. The "Brody Browne's" of education feel as helpless as the "Helene's", and more often than I like, they expect people like me to work miracles because:

You're the COUNSELOR." They say.

"Big Deal!!" I have to retort. "I'm the counselor, so what?" I look at a few books, read a little Psyche, and come up with a wad of theories about why people behave the way they do, and what I ought to do about it."

Well—If that's all it takes, I'd make sure that every black male like Ardro I talk to in school would graduate from college."

Ardro, like many of his friends, has an astounding intellect, but school has caused him nothing but trouble. Because of the mishmash of things at home, in school, and in the neighborhood, he barely finished 10th grade. He's been wobbling through 11th grade. Now just like his other friends, he's going to find that without school, no matter how many jobs he finds or how hard he works, he'll never be what he could have been, if he had completed—even high school. But there's been no telling him that. There's no getting Helene to understand that. In fact, there was no telling his friends, the police, the preacher, or anybody who knew him. Nobody cared! Not even Ardro!

After all the commotion died down, the discussions came to an end, and decisions were made. Ardro's fate was unceremoniously sealed. He and Helene were told that his education was put on hold. Suspended for a time—maybe for good.

He hardly blinked. As he faced his fate he didn't even realize the impact of what was about to happen to him. And not surprisingly, Helene was then, relieved that she didn't have to come back to that school again.

Therein lies the core of the mystery—"Why are there so few Caps and Gowns on the sturdy bodies of millions of Black Males?"

Ardro and his buddies like him are going to join the ranks of the unnumbered "ne'er do wells" of our society. When and if they do begin to realize their mistake, it's going to be too late.

With these brooding thoughts, Brody Browne and I miserably went home.

* * *

II

Running Scared

As fate would have it, Ardro was lucky. Early next morning, instead of being locked up like Michael, he was, in fact, suspended—not allowed back at school for two weeks. Everyday for the first week he was required to report to a JV counselor—his first brush with the penal system—who kept track of him. Then, without warning or explanation, he was detained at the JV center for three more days.

Reality then hit him brutally. Away from Helene for the first time, he was scared. Though her attention had always been disorganized, he missed her. And as he sat alone in a big room waiting to talk to the counselor, his mind raced with such erratic thoughts as:

"Man, I wonder if Momma knows where I am . . . I wish she was here . . . No I don't. All she'd be doing is crying, and I sure can't stand that. She's mad at me I know it. Ever since I was little, I felt like I was in the way. Maybe now she's glad I'm not there . . . . No she ain't. I know she loves me . . . . God, I wish I knew what's gonna happen! I wish Momma was here."

Though people were milling all about, for more than half-an-hour nobody even looked, or said anything to him. Every minute that passed he got more panicky. He tried. Then as he closed his eyes to shut out the truth of his situation, he laid his head against the wall, and he recalled Ms.Taylor—his third grade teacher. He remembered that it was she who had believed 'he was the greatest'. She wouldn't let him be scared when he had something new to do. She always told him how good he was. She made him feel safe.

He needed that safety now.

He thought about how, one time when he had written a story for Ms. Taylor, and she had asked him to read it for PTA one night. He thought about how he was scared to death to get up in front of people, and how Ms Taylor gave him a good "talking to." There, in his reverie he felt the pride. He did it, and was so thrilled. It seemed to him like she made him feel alive. She made the fear go away.

He needed that comfort now.

He painfully recalled that afternoon when he tried to tell Helene about the story he wrote for Ms. Taylor.

"Mom, Ms. Taylor says my story's good, and she wants me to read it at PTA."

"That's real good, Ardro. Now how you doing in Math?"

"Uh, O.K. I guess. You gonna come to PTA to hear my story?

"Yeah, I'm gonna try to make it. So much stuff goin' on, ya know."

But, that night at the PTA meeting he anxiously watched the door all evening, expecting to see Helene come in. She never showed.—

He felt someone walk close by. With a start, he opened his eyes. The fear came back. He figured she'd never show here either. "She don't care." He moaned. And in the next breath, "Oh, I wished she'd come!"

As he sat there, Ardro resumed his reflections. He then uneasily recalled to his time in 4th grade. What a difference! "That's when school got to be a bore." He recollected piteously. "That's the time I started to slack off."

He remembered telling Helene back then, "Momma, I wish Ms. Taylor was my teacher. Mr. Douglas don't pay any attention to me. Whenever I ask a question, he shuts me up. Then when I ask somebody else, he says I'm disturbing the class."

He cringed as he remembered Helene's wail in response. "Ardro, you know I don't like Mr. Douglas either. I told you that I had him when I was in the sixth grade. He was just as mean then, as he is now, and I can't face him again. Honey, you're just going to have to tough it out"

This, Ardro painfully remembered, is where he lost contact with school. Everybody was helpless. Everybody was scared. And there was nobody to make him feel like Ms. Taylor did. Ever since that time on, he had to do what Helene had told him—"tough it out", and then after that, he drifted, he played, he cheated, he fluttered and flopped through school.

Now, while he waited in the JV center, he was feeling sick. He wondered. "How much of this mess is my fault and how much is not?" He knew he had messed up on school. "How'd I get in this mess?" he searched his mind for answers.

His gloom drowned out the noises of the encircling crowd, and as his mind drifted off again, he closed his eyes. Then, as if in a dream, he relived the time he lost his skates. He experienced again, the last evening he asked his Momma for the roller blades.

As he harked back to what happened that night—his last big escapade, he recalled that Helene had known for some time that he had wanted a pair of roller blades. "They would give him a little ego boost," She thought—because getting them would make him do a little bit better in school. The cost however, of $75.00 was more than she could afford.

Though, at times it didn't seem like it, he always knew that Helene wanted to do more for him, but couldn't. He felt his burden on her, and regretted how her wanting to help him often backfired. He painfully thought. "I know Momma loves me, but it's hard for people like us to get money for things."

As his reverie continued, he clearly remembered Helene telling him, "I don't have it now, Ardro,"

"Well, ya' going to get it, ain't ya, Momma?" He pleaded.

"No, not before payday, that's for sure. You know we got to eat. You ain't got no job, so what am I gonna do?"

"Yeah, O.K. Momma." He sighed.

"Why doesn't somebody help?" He mourned silently. "Momma can't. I know she's tried. Nobody else cares."

It wasn't often that he asked for stuff like that, and his downhearted sigh made her feel awful.

After a long thoughtful pause, she said, "Well, maybe I can borrow it. I'll see tomorrow."

His enthusiastic grin was enough.

Next morning, she did something she really didn't want to do. She went downtown to the Fast Cash store, wrote a check for $100.00 and signed a piece of paper that said she would come in on payday to get the check back.

She took the money, went down to K-Mart, and bought a pair of roller blades for $79.95. It seemed easy. She'd seen many of her friends do the same thing. But little did she realize what would happen if she was late in recovering the check.

Helene was overjoyed that evening that Ardro was thrilled with his new toy. "Maybe that'll make him do better in school," she thought.

She watched him for a few minutes trying them out, and soon he skated out of sight. No cause for worry, she knew he'd be O.K. in the neighborhood. Within a half-hour after that, Ardro limped into the house screaming, "Momma, Call the police! Some strange dudes from down the street tackled me and took my skates off 'a me

Her roller coaster high, suddenly hit rock bottom.

He cringed as he remembered her yell. "Ardro, you dumb ass!" She screamed. "Why'd you let them kids do you like that?"

"I didn't let 'em, Momma." He cried. "I tried to get away, but them big guys caught me, and then I couldn't fight with the wheels on. Call the cops, Momma, please! Maybe they can find 'em."

She called them. And it brought her face-to-face with an ever-present factor of her social reality:—Attitudes.

Her first flush of anger with Ardro was quickly replaced with burning rage at the response of the police. When they came, they asked a few questions, wrote down what

Ardro told them, and then nonchalantly said, "We're never gonna find anything in this part of town. You know how it is. This happens all the time. By the time we track down those boys, the skates'll be sold to somebody else. Forget 'em. We can't do anything".

Neighbors, who were sitting on their steps, heard and saw the whole thing. They also heard what the cops had to say. Harshly and crudely, one of them said, "That kid didn't need them skates." Another, in defense, spoke-up and said, "Hush up. How'd you like that to happen to you?" Overhearing this conversation right after the police left, Helene was weak with despair. She slumped in the nearest chair to calm herself down.

Ardro didn't realize it at the time, but now in his predicament, he was beginning to understand the problems and the mystery that lie in the place in society commonly called "the lower social class." And his family suffers the consequences of the place. "Social position (social class) "Does that really have something to do with it?" He pondered then.

Actually, parents such as Helene, who realize that they are in the lower class, live and breathe the anxieties and frustrations of childcare. Many find it almost impossible to do more than feed, clothe and send the kids to school.

Consider the following:

He recalled that Helene glumly left him in the house, that awful evening, and walked alone down the street to St. John's, where she hoped to get a little comfort. She felt better as she sat there listening to the singing.

While she was there, one lady, not knowing that Helene was the boy's mother, stood up and started telling about the street incident.

"It's jus awful," She said. "Them older kids on the street don't belong in our neighborhood. And they don't respect nobody's property." I feel sorry for that kid. It just ain't right! Let's pray for 'im." And she started her prayer.

Other prayers were said, but after all the prayers, the preacher's remark was, "The Lord giveth, and the Lord taketh away. It must mean that that boy shouldn't have had them. He didn't need 'em!"

Without a word, Helene got up, dejectedly dashed out of the church, and started home to Ardro.

She passed her landlord on the way.

"Heard about ya boy." He said. "He O.K.?"

"Yeah, he's doing O.K. Mr. Mongus, I guess. Just shook up."

Without his knowing it, she overheard him mumble, as he walked away shaking his head, something like, "You ought to be paying your rent instead of buying that kind of stuff."

In his reverie, Ardro remembered it was dark when she got home. She sat mournfully alone on her steps for a few minutes before going into the house. He visualized her, solemnly watching TV sighing broodingly, "Nobody to turn to, and nobody to care."

He recalled her gloomy look at him; trying to sort out all the feelings that were hurting her; sadness, anger, pity and love for her child, but most of all sadness and frustration for her own plight.

As he waited there, in the JV center, he closed his eyes remembering that after several cheerless days Helene in her misery, forgot the date to "pay up" at Fast Cash, not realizing that every day she didn't go in added $6.31 to the bill. When she finally remembered to cover the check, the amount due was more than she expected she now owed $137.83—$24.00 more than she had in her purse. She started to write another check for the difference at an even higher interest rate, and then ruefully remembered what she had overheard the landlord mumble. Now realizing that she'd be late on rent again, she decided to expand the check to include another $150.00 to cover her rent shortfall.

The next day, she got the call that he, with two of his buddies had molested a girl at school and injured two teachers.

Now, all these things began to connect for Ardro. "Did the events of the last week, and the conditions in the community have anything to do with his participation in 'the attack'?"

"Here I am now," He mourned. "Sitting here alone in the JV center, anxiously waiting for my Mom, whose mind is frantic—more about our survival than about my future."

Ardro vaguely began to realize that Attitudes and Social Class do, indeed, have a lot to do with the mystery.

Ardro is one of millions of black males in the lower social class who encounters demeaning or patronizing attitudes from others in their communities.

In his particular community, consider the many middle class Black professionals and activists, including Mr. Mongus, their landlord, the real estate mogul and businessman in the city.

The Mongus family for example, really doesn't care about Ardro and his education in the same way they care about the education of their own son, Hugh, and the sons of their friends?

Look at the preacher, and the people of St. John's, the church where his mother goes. They don't care about or even know him.

His neighbors; they don't care about what he does as long as he doesn't annoy them.

Money and status are major factors.

Consider Ardro's Friend, Michael—one of the other boys involved in "the attack." Michael, too, is a black teen-ager, whose father is a well-to-do building contractor. Michael's parents were the first ones to rush in to Brody's office. Though his behavior was more violent than Ardro's, everybody's concern and consideration for him was greater than for Ardro. While there was nothing that Michael's parents could do, he knew that even though he had done wrong—(because he wanted to be like the boys)—he had their support. In his eyes, this was a novelty boyish incident. And very likely, when he gets out of jail, he'll be sent to another school to graduate.

In contrast, Ardro and Shirell, his other friend in the "attack," have only each other and their mothers—who are as helpless as they are—for support,

Why? Because their families, their neighborhood experience, their cultural background, their school performance, combined with their skin color, have relegated them to the lower place in society. And few other people have sincere interest in easing the conditions that keep them there because they are in—what most people call—a lower social class.

As we wrestle with these questions about Ardro, I realize that the same stories happen to thousands of Black youth every day in hundreds of schools, and communities. And the kids' fate is of little interest to almost everyone else they come in contact with. Many school counselors are afraid of them. Frustrated teachers give up on them. Parents are helpless and scared. The police are defensive and restrictive. The church is of no interest to them. They're usually put in classes with others just like them. There, most times, they become known as "them." Social services agencies, psychologists and Rehab programs test "them" and write prescriptions and proscriptions. To the community in general, "they" are a nuisance.

* * *

III

A Rude Awakening

Thus, we come back to Ardro, sitting alone in the JV center, pondering his past and his future. Like mine, his ruminations disappear—like fireworks in the sky at the end of the show; leaving only the smoke and smell of reality.

She finally came. Helene finally came in—so distraught, that she was crying and cursing. She had been held up because she had to go back to Fast Cash. She hadn't understood the fees she had to pay, and they were unforgiving. She now realized what a pickle she'd got herself into, and then she came into the center ticked off at Ardro, because he was the reason she went there in the first place. At that point all she could think of was that Ardro would have to go to work as soon as he got out, so she could pay-off Fast Cash.

Ardro felt sick. He wondered again how much of this mess was his fault and how much was not. Yeah, he had lost the skates, and also he had messed up on school, but now, "Why don't somebody help?" He moaned.

"Momma can't. I know she's tried. Nobody else cares!"

Mr. Buck, the JV counselor, who'd just joined them, informed Helene that Ardro would have to spend another three days in detention, and after investigation of "the attack" incident was complete, he would be on probation for six weeks. Only then would he be able to go back to school.

"Oh lordy" signed Ardro. The realization just hit him. For him, this was the beginning of the end of his formal education.

In order to keep him occupied while on probation Mr. Turner, his probation officer, took him over to the Home Display furniture store one day on the chance they would need someone to help load trucks.

What a day! After loading two large china cabinets, four heavy desks, four washing machines, a refrigerator and a bed room suite, the pain Ardro felt in his back and shoulders was worse than after a tough basketball game—worse than any he'd ever felt before. Hoping that Helene would rub his shoulders, he dragged himself home. Instead, as soon as he walked in the door, she started griping because she had to cook dinner for them after her hard day's work. Though he understood, he felt hot and bothered because she didn't pay any attention to him—or how he was feeling.

He bolted into his room. "I'm gettin' my butt out'a here tonight", he thought. "I don't have to go to school, so I ain't got no homework. I'm hittin' the street."

This flash of anger made him forget about the pain, until he bent down to pick up his pants. His yelp brought a thump on his door.

"Ardro, what ARE you doing in there? C'mon and eat."

Not answering, he grumpily went to the kitchen, yanked the chair out and slumped down. As he sat there, Helene gently patted him on the back and said,

"I know you're hurtin', Ardro. I am too. But, Honey, you're the only one I've got. I don't want to loose you.

Helene could see that he was fighting back tears. His anger, now replaced with sadness, he pleaded, "Momma, What am I going to do? I can't help you."

Overcome with pity for both of them, Helene just sat and looked at him. She didn't know how to answer. Then—not mindful that he desperately needed a hug, she strode out of the kitchen, where he just let his supper get cold on the plate in front of him.

The next morning, Ardro told, Mr. Turner, his probation officer about the night before. He couldn't find the words to describe how he was feeling, but for the first time, the officer sensed his feelings of helplessness.

"Ardro,—what—you're nearly sixteen now, aren't you? You're almost a man now. You've got to make it in a man's world. You know you almost blew your chances in school, and if you don't go back to school now, when this is over, you'll ruin the only chance you have is to find a respectable job."

"I can't go back to school now," he moaned. "I'm too far behind, Mr. Turner. I'm sure to flunk. I'll be the 11th grade dummy next year, and I can't stand them teachers looking at me like I don't belong there. Besides, My Momma wants me to try to help her."

"Well then, Ardro," Mr. Turner admonished. "You can't just loaf. You've got to find some kind of a job."

"Uhmm," He considered. "Well working at Home Display ain't for me. I'm not a big guy. I can't handle that heavy stuff every day, but . . . I guess I'll have to find something." Then as an afterthought, Ardro groaned. "Heck, I can't even join the Army. I'm not old enough yet, and I couldn't even pass the test. What am I going to do?" He moaned.

Mr. Turner simply said, "Get a job Ardro."

"Do I have to do Home Depot tomorrow?

"No, Ardro. You do seem like a good fellow. You just stay here in the office and run errands for the next two days. Don't think you're going to loaf, though. We're going to keep you busy."

On the third morning, Helene stopped in to see him. He was glad to see her. Although he was busy, they had a short quiet chat before she had to leave. About mid-afternoon that day, Mr. Turner, and a deputy came in to tell that he was released to go home. He felt scared for a moment. This was a brand new time in his life. No school, no job, on probation, and nobody to talk to.

Tired, and dejected, he walked out of the JV office, and dismally strolled toward his street.

As he ambled on his way back home, he heard music. It got his attention, because it was coming from a house where one of his mother's friends lived. Miss Tina went to the same church, and several times she would stop at his house after church to chat with Helene. On impulse, we walked up to the door and knocked on it. Instead of Miss Tina, a young girl answered the door.

"Yeah, what do ya want?"

"Well, uh, I was looking for Miss Tina."

"She's not here—. Hey, don't you stay with Miss Helene, up the street?"

"Yeah, she's my Mom."

"O.K., Tina's my Mom. She had to go to the store. You can come in and wait for her if you want."

Ardro thought, "Boy! This is a pretty chick. Maybe I'll stick around for a few minutes. I ain't got nothing to do."

"Uh, O.K. for a little while, if it's O.K. with you." He said timidly.

When he got inside the house he could see that she was indeed a very attractive young woman—probably older than he was. The house was neat and clean, and the music was the kind that he liked. It sounded like he felt—soulful and sad. He was uneasy, but he spied a chair in the corner and he sat down.

"What's your name," he hesitantly asked.

"Bernetta. What's yours?"

"Ardro." He felt funny, talking to a girl all alone in her house.

She was quiet for a minute, and then she abruptly asked, "Ardro, why are you out of school today? You sick or something?"

"Nah, I quit." Just spilled out of his mouth.

Suddenly, he felt ashamed, and he jumped up and bolted toward the door. "It's started already," he thought.

Bernetta stopped him.

"Hey, Arglow, what's the rush?"

"My name's ArDRO, and I ain't in no rush." In his weak attempt to pass her, then he said, "And I'm just upset."

"O.K., O.K. Ardro. If you want to talk to my Mom about it, she'll be back in a few minutes. Just sit down and relax . . . . You like that song that's playing?"

"Um hum, it's pretty." He began to calm down. "That's what made me stop in." And with an admiring glance said, "I'm glad you're here."

"I'm glad you're here too, Ardro." Sympathetically she said, "Looks like you need some cheering up. What the matter?"

"I got kicked out of school a few days ago." He admitted. "They told me I could come back in six weeks . . . but I can't go back. It's a long story."

Then Bernetta said something that bowled him over. "Ardro, I know how you feel. Ardro, I dropped out of school too. My story's probably just as long as yours, but we can't give up. You ought'n to quit, You oughta go back."

"Yeah." Eyeing her steadily and nodding, "You're probably right." He began to feel more at ease. "You know Bernetta; I don't really remember seein' you at school. How come?"

"Hmm,—Ardro, that's part of the story. We'll have to talk about it."

All this time Ardro kept thinking, "Wow! This is a pretty girl, and she seems really nice. I could really like her."

"Well, can I come back sometime?"

Then as he opened his mouth to say something else, they heard Miss Tina coming in the door.

"Ardro! How you doin' boy? What ya doin' here? Helene sick or somethin'?"

No Miss Tina, I was just goin' by, and heard some music. Just stopped in to say Hi. Momma's at work. She's doin' O.K. Since I'm out of school today, I was just walking. Don't get mad with Bernetta for lettin' me in. I'm glad she did."

After a few minutes of chatting with Miss Tina, Ardro then said, "Well, good to see you, Miss Tina. I gotta be goin' now." And with a glance at Bernetta, "Can I come back sometime?"

"Anytime you feel like it, honey, come on over. Tell your Momma, Hi. I'll see her at church."

Now, He felt a LOT better. "There's somebody in the world that knows what I feel like." he thought. His feet didn't feel nearly as heavy as they did before, and they carried him home in a blur.

As soon as he got in the house, he turned on the radio, and was trying to find the station that played that song he and Bernetta had listened to at her house. Very soon after, Helene elbowed her way through the door with her arms full of groceries.

"Ardro, c'mere 'n help me," she called. I got some good news for you, "and Baby, I'm feelin' good!"

Surprised to hear Helene so happy, he rushed over to grab a couple of the bags. "Momma, what's up?" he asked. It was good to see her in such high spirits.

"Well, boy, I got paid today, and on the way home I stopped by the Chopper shop; you know, that little store that sells cards. I didn't know it, but in there they sell lotto tickets—the two-dollar scratch-off kind. I bought one, and guess what happened. I still can't believe it—I won $750.00!"

"Oh, Momma!!!"

"Yes, and it only cost me two dollars. Ain't it great? Praise the Lord!!!

She was giggling and crying at the same time. "Praise the Lord!" She shrieked again. Ardro was speechless. He just grinned as he watched her.

"And Ardro, you know what I did? I went straight down to that Fast Cash store, and told'em I had their money. That lady looked at me kind'a funny, and then started punchin' in numbers on her machine, and then 'Old Stoneface' threw me a piece of paper, that she called a 'statement'. That piece of paper said that I owed them $320.00. I almost fell on the floor, but Ardro, I paid it."

"But Momma, you only borrowed One Hundred, and you paid them back more than that already"

"Yeah, but Honey"—She explained—"the rent had to be paid, so I got some more. I couldn't ever catch up, but thank God, I got'em today."

"And now ya' got some money left over.—Alright!!"

For the first time in a long time they both felt more than a little happiness.

Helene turned to go to the kitchen. "I'm goin' to cook us some food," she said, and then she whirled around and came back.

"Ardro, I'm sorry, I been ramblin' on every since I came in—"Now it's your turn."—In rapid-fire order—"Tell me, what's goin'on with you? What did the counselor say? What did you do this afternoon?"

He paused. He had to collect his thoughts. The change of subject threw him for a minute. "Well uh, Momma, Mr. Turner told me I oughta go back to school when they let me."

Already, he began to feel his moment of cheer draining out of him. He haltingly told Helene about his thoughts of dropping out.

"I can't go back there now, Momma." He whimpered. "I know I'm gonna flunk! I'm too far behind. Next year, the kids'll be laughin' at me if I'm only in the 11th grade. I can't! I can't go back. I'll just have to get some kind'a job." He was not defiant. He was hurt, and he could feel hot tears in his eyes.

Then he brightened as he recalled the other part of his afternoon.

"On the way home I stopped by Miss Tina's. She wasn't there, but Bernetta was. Boy, she's pretty! We listened to some music and had a few words. That's all. Then Miss Tina came in. She told me to tell you, 'Hi!' and Bernetta said I could come back sometime. Boy She's pretty!"

Helene listened to Ardro, and felt his pain as he talked of dropping out of school, and of having to go to work to help her. Almost at the same time, she was alarmed at the other part of his story. She didn't know Miss Tina very well, but she did know—or thought she did—about Bernetta. Neighborhood gossip had got back to her, and her mother instinct kicked in. "I'm gonna find out for sure" she said to herself, as she hugged her boy, held him close, and shuffled off into the kitchen.

Just then, Ardro heard something he hadn't heard for a long time—the telephone. "Umm, Momma must have paid the bill, "he thought as he reached over to grab it. It was Shacky, an older school buddy who dropped out in the 10th grade. Up to that time Shacky had been a year ahead of him.

"Hey Ardro, You O.K? I heard you ain't in school. What'cha doin?"

"I don't know, Shack. Right now I'm just tryin' to make up my mind. In a little while I might be out there with you. How you doin?"

"Not good,—but at least I don't have to sit in that stupit school where nobody wants me, and be bored stiff. I got a job at the Pizza Bar, makin' a couple of extra bucks." Thinkin' 'bout a lot of other stuff too. I wanna talk to ya."

"Yeah, well I understand, Shack. Like I said, I might be out there wit' ya' buddy. I don't know what's gonna happen. Right now though, I got too many things to think about."

Although he was glad to hear from Shacky, he didn't feel much like talking at that time. So after a short chat, he said, "Well Shack, uh I Gotta go now, Shack, Call me again sometime. See ya. Momma wants me to do something."

"O.K. Ardro. Call me when ya' get a chance. Bye"

Helene was humming something soft and sweet when Ardro went back in the kitchen—she often did that when she was thinking. She stopped mixing the biscuit dough, and looked at him and said, "Boy, how well do you know Bernetta?"

Caught off guard, He answered. "I just met her, Momma—today. Well maybe I've seen her on the street. But today's the first time I knew who she is, and what she really looks like."

"Ya know she's older than you are, don't ya"

"Well, I kinda figured that, but she seems like a nice girl—Ain't she?

"Oh Yeah, she's a real nice girl. Miss Tina's done a good job of raisin' her,—But Ardro, I ain't sure about something.—I just don't want so see you get your hopes up, and then be real disappointed. I gotta find out something for sure."

By now Ardro really felt confused. "What's Momma talking about? He thought. "Oh Lord, I hope that chick ain't got AIDS or somthin'!" He went back to the front room, turned on the radio, and sure enough, THAT song was playing again—the one he had heard with Bernetta over at Miss Tina's house. When it went off, the DJ announced its title, "The End of Delight".

"Ah! Man, that was so pretty," he sighed, "I wish it would play again." but he knew that on the radio that doesn't happen. So he trudged back to the kitchen. He dawdled there for a minute before saying to Helene, "Momma, can I go down to the store and buy a tape? I've got $7.00 left over from my pay. That was a pretty song I was listening to, and I want the tape. I heard it over at Bernetta's and I want it."

She felt a flutter again, but the only thing she could say was, "O.K., but don't stay out too long. Hurry back Ardro, supper's almost ready."

He flew out the door. And just as soon as he left, Helene picked up the phone and called Mazie Cox, the neighbor everybody calls the "town crier".

"Mazie would know", she thought, "She knows everything about everybody. And most of the time Mazie's right!"

After a five-minute chat with Mazie, Helene had the "dirt";—Proof of what she had thought all along. She felt bad, but now she felt compelled to reveal something to Ardro that she knew he didn't want to hear. She hoped and prayed that he would be able to handle it O.K.

In about twenty minutes he came rushing back, and just before he started the tape player, she called him.

"Come on Honey, dinner's ready, and gettin' cold. C'mon let's eat."

Ardro enjoyed his dinner. He wolfed it down in a hurry—hoping to get back to listening to his new recording. He hardly listened to Helene, who was chattering all the time about school, finding a job and about finding a girl friend. He didn't want to think about it just now, he was thinking about Bernetta and the song they liked.

Then Helene abruptly interrupted his reflections, and asked again.

"What do you know about Bernetta, Ardro? You sure you never heard any of the boys talkin' 'bout her?"

"No, Momma, why should I? I just met her today. She seems so nice, and we seem to hit it off real good. I like her—What's up?

Helene drew a heavy sigh, and then—"Ardro, Like I said,—Bernetta's a nice girl, but don't put your hopes on makin'-out with her. I know she might like to be your friend, but—not many people know this—but that girl don't want no man. She don't look like a man, but she sure don't want to sleep with one. If you ever do find a good woman, she might fight you for her.

Ardro didn't move a muscle. He just sat there stricken. "This can't be real. Momma's just making this up," He thought. I know she don't want me to drop out of school and get some girl pregnant. Maybe that's why she's sayin' this."

Helene jarred him out of his stupor, "Ardro, did ya hear me?"

I don't like tellin' you this, Ardro, but I'd rather you find it out now than later someplace else.

"Damn, Momma, you tellin' me that Bernetta's a—?" He couldn't say it.

"Ardro, I ain't tellin' you what she is; I'm telling'ya what peoples' sayin, 'bout her. And from what I been told, she's chasin' all the high school girls around here that'll pay her any attention. They tell their mommas about it.—So Ardro, take it easy. Please—don't fall for somebody you can't have!"

His only answer to Helene, as he slowly got up from the table was, "O.K Mom"

He felt numb. All his feelings of hope for love and fulfillment were fading away. His mind was raging, "This can't be real. I don't have anybody to talk to about it. Why does this kinda stuff have to happen to me? I know Momma ain't makin' this up, but maybe, just maybe—Nah.—This just ain't right!!! That girl wants to talk to me. Should I? Momma's always talkin' about God. Is God goin' to let this happen to me—just when

I thought I might find somebody who cares?—Well, I know she cares, but what if I fall in love????? What if??? Oh, Lord, What am I gonna do?"

He went straight to his tape player, and put in the new recording he bought, and found the right track. It was then that the song title, "The End of Delight" had violent and horrendous meaning for him, As He sat and listened once more to it; misery tore through him and began to take away the only hope he had.

Helene stood watching him. She ached for him as she saw his wretchedness. "It's not just this news about Bernetta," she thought, "but all the other stuff he's facing." "God, I hope he's going to make it O.K.!!"

"Momma, Why's it got to be like this? He said, with disgust. It seems like nothin' I do is right. Why can't you and me be happy?"

"We got each other," Helene said with gloomy passion, "and that's all that counts."

"To you maybe, but I want more," He ranted. "I want more! I want a job where I can make money for us. I want to go back to school. I want a girl I can call mine. And now, the way it looks I ain't gonna have none of it." He sat down, filled with despair, in the chair. And for the next half-hour he just stared at the wall, while Helene washed the dishes.

She hummed her melancholy tune. Then as she thought about Ardro, and about what he might do now, all of a sudden she heard the front door slam. Her heart skipped a beat as she flew to the door to see which way he went. "Oh God, don't let him do nothing crazy," she groaned.

Ardro, trying to escape his angry passion was running. Running just as hard as he could. He could actually feel the thump, thump of his heart pumping. It felt good—really good until . . . suddenly he fell exhausted in the grass between the curb and the sidewalk. He lay there several minutes moaning aloud; not really understanding his torment.

When he eventually got himself together, he realized that three boys were standing over him. As he studied their faces he recognized one of them as Shacky, the guy he had just talked to today.

"Hey Ardro, What's up?" Shacky—seeming a long way off—asked. "What's the matter wit'chu?"

The guys helped Ardro sit up, but he was afraid to try to stand up, because he felt sick. "Hi Shack," he said weakly. "I'm O.K; Just a little shook-up. I ain't had no good news for many a day, and today didn't help a bit." He couldn't bring himself to say anything about Bernetta, though he was dying to know if they had ever heard anything.

"Man, you sure look like you need a lift," said Shacky. "I don't know what's jaggin' ya, but you gotta get over it. C'mon lets go over to the club," He urged, "'n git this mess off your mind.—Hey guys, how 'bout we give him a lift. You know—he just might be a good partner some day?"

Ardro didn't want to think about the next few minutes. All he wanted to do was just sit there on the make-shift stool, get himself together, and then take a long walk.

"No, Shack," He begged off. "I'm goin' home in a few minutes. Just let me be. I'll be O.K."

"Aw, c'mon guy, we ain't goin' to leave ya sittin' here," they said. "We'll take good care of ya. Git up and come on wid us."

Gingerly he slowly got to his feet. Shacky grabbed his arm, and held on to him as they guided him past several storefronts, and a church. With his head was still reeling, he could smell the springtime flowers on the trees. He recalled that same fragrance that filled the air when he used to walk to school. "Hmm, I wonder where I am?" He mused. He let himself be guided along for several minutes.

Soon they approached an old house. Richie, one of the guys, said he lived there. "Why are we goin' here?" Ardro asked. They mumbled an answer, He felt uneasy as they led him through a door with colored lights behind it. The only one of the guys Ardro actually knew was Shacky, and he knew this wasn't his house.

He turned, and attempted to leave, when from somewhere inside he heard music. He froze. The song that was playing in a distant room was "The End of Delight".

"Where's that music?"—His heart raced like crazy.

"Down the hall", said Shacky. "C'mon in and relax. You need a lift."

"Yeah, that music—it really hits me!" He wanted to go in, but at the same time he wanted to leave—"It sounds so nice." He sighed.

"Yeah, they play pretty music here." Shacky said. "C'mon in and listen. You'll like it. This is a fine place—a great place to hangout. If you like what's here, you can come anytime you want."

Warily, Ardro entered with them into a room that had the look and feel of a large plush family room. Several lamps cast a rosy glow over the whole room, which held several tables, sofas and soft chairs. He spied a sofa across the room, went and sat down heavily. The others chose to sit at a nearby table; leaving him to his music and his thoughts.

Though he didn't know where the music that softly filled the room was coming from, he slowly began to relax. Feeling better, he became more alert, and as another song was playing, he noticed the three boys in heavy conversation. They seemed to be ignoring him, and he didn't care.

"Hmm, this ain't bad," he thought. The music, intermingled with the titillating laughter of the waitress behind the bar, was delightful.

Then Shacky interrupted. "Ardro, c'mon over and sit wid us. You want somthin' to drink?"

"Nah Shack. Thanks, but I ain't got no money with me, I can't get nothin' now."

"Aw hell Man, don't worry 'bout that. We'll hook you up. What kinda drink ya want?"

"Well,"—He hesitated—"O. K. Just a Coke or Pepsi of somthin' like that."

"That's all???"

"Yep, that's all, then I gotta go home. Momma's worried about me."

Shacky leaned back, shook his head and said, "O.K."

Then he yelled, "Hey, Angie, Fix Ardro one o' them cola's. Put a little o' ya' sweet sunshine in it."

Unaware of the content of the order, Ardro missed the clue. Without hesitation he began to sip the drink that looked like a regular cola. It was nice and cold, and it gave him a lift as it trickled down his gullet. It was refreshing.

Then after he finished, he suddenly thought about Helene worrying about him, and got up to leave.

One of the guys yelled, "Hey man, where you going?"

"I told ya, man, I gotta go home. I know Momma's worried about me. She didn't know I was goin' out,"

"Thanks, Shack, for you guys picking me up. I was having a hard time, but I'm better now. I gotta go. See ya later!—Oh,—Somebody show me how to get outa here"

Shacky quickly got up from the table, and led him through the hallway and the front door. Then as Ardro walked away, he said, "You'll be O.K. Ardro, don't worry, you'll be O.K."

Once again, Ardro's feet felt light, but this time he was aware of it. To him it seemed like he was floating along the sidewalk. He could feel his chest expanding, and he experienced the sense of hearing a strange whistling sound, like a teakettle boiling. As he floated, he got hot from the steam he seemed to be passing through. It wasn't unpleasant, and he delighted in the imaginary smell of Bernetta's perfume as he whizzed past her.

When he finally came out of this flight of imagination, he wasn't exactly sure of where he was, but he began to see some familiar places, then, strangely happy, he hummed the tune, "The End of Delight" all the way to his street.

As he turned the corner to go to his house, it started again. This time, he felt a thump in the middle of his chest. It slowed him down. He wasn't floating anymore. The thump came again, and again, and then it seemed to linger and get heavy—right in the middle of his chest. This new weight seemed to slow him down even more. To Ardro, it seemed as though he was plodding through the thickest mud he had ever imagined—mud up to his knees. It was taking all his effort to move, and he began to sweat. He noticed that his heart was racing, and it took all his effort to breathe.

He panicked when he realized that he hadn't gone more than 10 paces since this all started, and he tried to yell for Helene. Nothing came out of his mouth.

"Oh good God, wha's hap'nin?" he thought. "Oh, Mamma, come out, please come out!"

He hadn't realized it, but he had come to a standstill. One of the neighbors, Ms. Delores, several doors up the street, saw him standing there and wondered, "Why in the world is Ardro just standing there in the street this time of the night?" She stood on her porch and watched him. He didn't move. She called to him. He didn't answer. Then, not knowing what was happening, she cautiously, walked toward him, calling his name. Not getting a response, she touched him—a couple of times.

Ardro, meanwhile, was tranced-out—calling desperately for Helene, and slogging through that heavy mud with every muscle in his body aching. He was not aware of the approach of Ms. Delores until she firmly grabbed him. Then her touch jarred him into action, and he screamed. She knew then that he was in trouble, so she took his hand, and he let her gently lead him toward his house.

"I'm getting him home to his Momma," she thought. "Something's real wrong." Though she had watched him stand motionless for almost five minutes, she could see that he was in a cold sweat, and she thought that was odd, especially since he wasn't moving—just standing there.

"Helene! Helene!!" she called. "Open the door! Open the door, something's wrong with your boy. And then she was startled. Ardro began to sing.

By this time Ardro was floating again. He could feel his shirt flapping in the wind, and the air taking his breath away. The streetlights and the car lights were beautiful brilliant colors, which were just flashing by. This all filled his racing heart with joy that he had never known before.

When Helene saw him, she screamed. "Oh my God, Oh Good Lord, what's wrong with m'boy?" Her heart fell when she saw his eyes. They were empty. She and Ms. Delores sat him down in a chair, and she could feel his heart thumping real hard. He was wringing wet with sweat, and the only sound she could hear was heavy, heavy breathing—then a deep groan when he appeared to fall into a sound sleep.

At first, she thought he might be drunk, but when she leaned over to smell his breath, there was no odor. As she did so, he leaped out of the chair, and fell to the floor with both hands over his chest, as if in deep pain. Then he yelped, and she was sure he was indeed in pain.

"Delores, call 911. He's dying. He's dying!!! Oh My God!!!"

In 30 minutes, Medics were carrying Ardro out to a waiting ambulance. In that time, and with a remarkable assortment of instruments, they had determined that Ardro was not dead, but was suffering from a kind of heart failure. They were puzzled, because they had never seen so young a patient in this condition.

Ms. Delores calmed Helene as she helped her walk out of the house to the front seat of the ambulance. Helene was distraught and confused. She could barely answer the Medic's questions. All they could get out of her was that he had been out, she didn't know where, and that the neighbor brought him home in this shocking state.

"He's got hold of something, He's in bad shape." They said as they took him out the door. They left to go immediately to the County Hospital. Helene sobbed through it all until a doctor approached the gurney where Ardro was stretched out.

"What's the matter with him Doctor?" She moaned. "Wha's the matter with my boy?" A nurse sat her down and comforted her while the doctor did his examination.

It seemed forever for Helene. Then the doctor soberly walked up to her and began to explain something he called a "Psychedelic psychosis".

"A sack o' what?"

"Psy ki del ik," the doctor slowly re-pronounced. "A Psychedelic Psy-ko sis, which means he's eaten or had something to drink that causes people to have nightmares and visions—we call it hallucinations—unreal, scary or pleasurable imaginations."

"It also causes the blood pressure to go up, and there are other physical effects that he's not used to."

"Has he ever had trouble with his heart? He asked.

"Lord, No" She wailed. "Why? Did he have a heart attack?"

"No", the doctor explained. "We don't think so; he's too young for that—if that's all that happened to him.—He came pretty close though. Whatever he got, the dose was pretty powerful, especially for a kid his age. I believe he's been messing with somebody who gave him LSD—the kids call it 'Acid'."

"Oh my God! Moaned Helene!"

By this time Ardro had gone to sleep. Helene watched him snore peacefully. He lay this way for almost an hour. She began to relax, and after a few minutes nap, she had begun to think of going home and leaving him till morning.

Suddenly, lying motionless flat on his back, He began to cry out loud, and then he began to yell. To him—He was angry. He was at school, chasing some kid through the hall. Though he couldn't feel it, they both were running on shards of glass and their blood was splashing on the walls. He could see Ms. Taylor, his Third grade teacher, standing at the end of the hall, and before he knew it he had run through her as through air—dashing headlong into the wall behind where she stood. Lightning struck him in the same instant, and he felt his heart stop.

Just as Helene was about to leave the room she heard his yell—and then a heavy groan. She turned to look at Ardro. He looked stretched out, and was as rigid as a board. His eyes were wide open and she heard a growl that seemed to come from deep inside him. She thought, "My God, he's havin' a fit!"

When she screamed for the doctor, a nurse rushed in, and even before she had secured him to the bed, a team of attendants and a doctor hurriedly set to work.

"Ardro! Ardro!" The doctor called. "Wake up. Wake up—can you tell me what's happening?"

When he got no response the doctor anxiously placed his stethoscope on Ardro's chest, and listened in amazement to what sounded like an idling heavy diesel truck motor. The musky heat he felt from Ardro's body made him step back. He knew then that Ardro had far exceeded his tolerance level for whatever he had taken.

Meanwhile Helene was crying, "Ardro honey, what have you done? Oh, my baby, please don't die!" The doctor and his staff speedily discussed their next step. They decided to give him an injection. That soon began to relax him.

"Your boy's in real trouble," he soberly told Helene. "We still don't know what, or how much he's had, or how he got it. It won't do any good to pump his stomach because it's in his nervous system now. We'll just have to wait to see whether his heart can stand the strain; and his heart's our main concern. Other than his heart, he's a strong boy, and he should come through this O.K."

"Come on, Mrs. Knight; let one of the nurses take you back to the lounge. You can wait there for a while until we can get more of a handle on this. We'll let you know how things are as soon as we can."

Helene reluctantly left the emergency room. She was desolate. As she sat alone in a corner of the lounge she prayed:

"Jesus! My Dear Lord, please, please don't take my child away! He's all I got. I want him to be happy again. He was so unhappy 'bout school 'n everything. He was so scared. He wanted to grow up, and NONE of it ever went right for him. I don't know how to help him, and I ain't got nobody to help me. Please, God, Make 'im well again. Give 'im another chance and, Dear Lord, help me to find a way to get him to go back to school."—

ARDRO'S REVIVAL

While she prayed, Ardro started his long road back to reality. He felt the sharp prick of the doctor's needle, and he wondered where he was. All the voices around him were too loud, but they were making sense. They were talking about some guy who was having heart problems. Then he heard his name.

"Ardro!" somebody called. "Ardro, Say something to me—are you alright?" He tried to answer, but his tongue wouldn't work right.

"Huhnnn," he uttered as he stared at the strange face of a doctor he'd never seen before. This scared him, and at the same time it brought him more contact with reality. He knew now, that he was the guy they had been talking about.

"How'd I get here?" He mumbled, and he tried to get up.

They gently restrained and tried to reassure him. "Hey Ardro, lay still. You're O.K. You're in the hospital. Your mother's here with you, and we're trying to help you."

"What happened?" he inquired, "Why am I here?"

"We don't know. You're going to have tell us. Right now, the only thing you can do is relax."

His mouth felt like it had wax in it. "Momma! Where's Momma? I wanna see her." Seeing her, he felt, would help him sort out what's real and what's the other stuff that's been going on. "Please go get 'er."

He was breathing normally now, but he had a horrific headache and felt lightheaded. When they escorted Helene into the room, she had settled down, and was smiling. She rushed over to Ardro, almost afraid to touch him, but with her first sight of him, she realized that he was indeed back. His eyes were bright and shiny, and she knew that he recognized her, Her heart leaped for joy.

She heaved a sigh, "Thank you Lord!"—Then, "Ardro, what happened honey?"

Again, he tried to speak, but what he said was faint and indistinct. His tongue still felt numb as he tried to tell Helene how glad he was to see her, but it was hard for him to form words.

"Damn, I can't talk," he thought, and he began to get restless.

The doctor spoke firmly, "Everything's O.K. Ardro. Just relax, and it's going to get all right. You can go to sleep now."

He turned to Helene, "Ms. Knight, I think you ought to stick around for a while yet. He's going to need reassurance when he wakes up. Also, you can help us find out from him what he remembers. We've got to know how he got the stuff in him, and where he got it. LSD, if that's what it is, is dangerous, and we don't want anyone else to get it if we can help it. We'll call you again from the lounge when he wakes up. You try to get some sleep yourself."

"Alright, Doctor, said Helene, I'm fine now. Thank You."

Ardro slept for more than three hours. He woke up confused and disoriented, and it took him a few minutes to realize that he wasn't in his own bed. When he started to get up he realized that a man was standing beside him. He flinched.

"Ardro, I'm a nurse," the man said quietly, "and you're in the hospital."

"Your mother is out in the lounge, waiting for you to wake up. Just rest a bit, and the doctor will be here shortly. Then we'll call her."

The doctor, now tired from a long night's work, breathed a sigh of relief when he saw Ardro. "Ardro," he said gustily, "I think you've made it. It was touch and go there, for a while. I don't know how, but you got hold of some very bad stuff, somewhere, somehow, and it almost did you in."

What d'ya mean, Doctor?

"I mean that you've had a "bad trip" that almost killed you. Where did you get LSD, or 'acid', or whatever you kids call it?"

"Uh, I don't know what you're talkin' about. I haven't been on no trip, and I never mess with 'acid'". Ardro was really bewildered.

"Well, somehow, you got a good dose of 'acid' in you, and you almost had a heart attack"

"Acid? Acid!! Oh my God, Shac—??? He stopped in mid-sentence.

"Where's Momma?" I gotta ask her somethin'." He felt a cold chill. "She's here ain't she?"

"She's on her way down here now, Ardro," said one of the nurses. "Take it easy. She'll be here in a minute."

His mind was racing, "What did I do? I just remember being with the guys at that club they call the Orchid Club—listenin' to music. I didn't smoke nothin'. I didn't eat nothin'. What happened?"

"Ardro, Ardro. You're O.K. Praise the Lord!!" Helene cried as she dashed into the room. She pushed the nurses aside as she grabbed and held Ardro close. "Oh, I'm so glad you're back."

She could feel that he was about ready to cry. "What's the matter, Child?"

"Momma, what's the matter with me?" Ardro asked. "The doctor's was talking about me getting a heart attack from 'acid' or somethin'. You know I don't mess with that stuff. What are they talking about?"

"Honey, I don't know. All I know is that you were nearly crazy, and you nearly died. You got something someplace, and they're trying to find out where. Where'd you go? I know you were upset when you went out. What happened?"

"Well"—He thought for a long minute.—"You know, Momma, When you told me about Bernetta, I got blasted. It blowed me away! I just couldn't sit still, so I got up and I ran outside, and I just started running—'til I fell down. I don't know where I was, but while I was still on the ground, a bunch of guys came up to me and started talkin'. Shacky was with 'em."

"We sat there on the side of the street, just talkin' for a while, and then they said they was gonna to take me to someplace to relax. Well—I don't know which way we went, but after a pretty good little hike, we came to this big old house."

He paused, trying to collect his thoughts. "We went in this house. It was kinda' nice in there, Momma—fixed up like a club in one of the big rooms." He mused.

"Ardro, What was there? "Who was there?" Asked the doctor.

"I don't really know. There were only a few people there, but, all I can remember is this lady, Momma—a real big lady. She sure was pretty, but she musta weighed 400 pounds, and she was awful nice. Shacky called her Angie—yeah, Angie's what they called 'er."

"An what did she do?" asked Helene, "Did you talk to her?"

"No, I didn't talk to her. She was just takin' care of the bar and waitin' on tables, laughin' and talkin' to everbody; servin' drinks and stuff."

"Well, who was with you?" Insisted Helene.

"Uh, Shacky was with me, and three or four other guys. One of them said his name was Richie. Yeah, Richie—He even said it was his house. I wasn't feelin' good and I was sittin' on a sofa, but they was all sittin' at a table talking'."

He recalled wondering that they were talking about. "Were they talkin' 'bout him?" He shook his head, trying to get the cobwebs out.

Then the doctor broke through his thoughts, "Ardro, did you drink anything?"

"No, not then." He shook his head, then—"Uh . . . yeah . . . Yeah! Shack did call me over to the table, and ask me if I wanted a drink. I told 'm no, 'cause I didn't have no money. But, since I was so low the guys kept buggin' me to get a drink because, they thought I needed a lift."

"Well, did they give you one?"

"Uh-huh, Yeah, I told'm I'd take a coke; Maybe that'd make me feel a little bit better. So Shack called Angie over. Angie had been laughing and talking with some other people, so he told her to put a little bit of her sunshine in it, 'cause I needed some sunshine in my life."

"Sunshine!!" The doctor blurted. "Sunshine! Ardro, have you ever heard of yellow sunshine?"

"Umm, yeah, yeah!" Ardro closed his eyes. Then his eyes widened in alarm, he recalled one of his friends getting some stuff they called yellow sunshine at a party. "Oh, good God! That's that stuff that people say makes you go nuts." He shouted. One had told him that it was fun. But he knew one of the girls that went crazy for a while.

"I ain't had none o' that, have I?" "How'd I get it?" Ardro wailed.

"Oh, yes you have," said the doctor. "It was probably in, or on, that glass you drank that coke out of." "Ardro, you just said. Angie was told to give you some sunshine. Could that be it?"

This time, he completed his exclamation, "Oh, My God! Shack!! How? Why?"

At that, Helene got blazing mad! But then after recalling the friendship of Shacky and Ardro from a couple of years before, she softened.

"Oh Ardro, please don't say Shacky did it. He seem like such a nice boy." Then she reconsidered. He never liked school and dropped out, and also, she knew that he had taken up with a lot of other boys in the street—doing God knows what.

"Oh, Good Lord, what if he did? I gotta go see his Mom. I gotta find out if this is real."

"No, Momma, don't do that. Lemme go 'n talk to 'im when I get outta here. I gotta find out why he did somethin' like that to me—if he did." And with rising agitation, "And if he did, I wanna straighten 'im out"

"No, Baby! Let it be. I'm ready to call the police now, and let them handle it. There's too much of that kind of stuff happening in this area. Maybe now, I can get somebody to do somethin' around here. I'm sick and tired of seeing kids getting hurt, and killed and,—and—!" She was losing her composure.

The doctor intervened. "Ardro, your Momma's right. This is something that the police ought to know. We can give them this information, and they'll find out who's responsible, and where this place is." He continued, "Ardro, you're lucky to be alive. Some other kids get away with it, but whether you know it or not, you have a heart that can't stand the kind of stress you just went through."

"Ya mean, I oughta jus' let the cops handle it?"

"Yes, Ardro!" Helene shouted

"Yes," repeated the doctor. It won't be good for you to get more involved.

The hospital notified the police authorities of the incident.

"Well Doctor, What do you expect us to do about it?" Said the police officer that showed up. "There must be 20 or 30 of these houses in the city, and every time we shut one house down another one pops up. We put one person in jail, and somebody else comes along."

The Doctor nodded, because he understood the situation all too well. "But," he insisted, "These places are a menace to the whole area, officer. Please go find that house, and arrest those people. They almost killed a boy, and chances are, another boy or girl is going to die from acid, drugs or something else that they are selling over there—wherever it is."

Exasperated, the officer said, "O.K. Doc. We'll go find that house, and we'll put' em in jail. But Doctor," He shouted. "We can't save those kids."

"Most of those boys don't want anything. They won't go to school, and they ain't worth nothing. We're busy trying to protect the people's property that they're out there stealing. They're keeping us busy putting them in jail just for that!"

The doctor started to respond, but just then he was called to another patient.

"O.K. Officer, but please get those people. They nearly killed this boy. Thank you."

Helene listened to this conversation in amazement. She didn't say anything, but she was boiling mad as she watched the policemen walk out of the hospital.

"How could that cop say my boy's no good? He don't even know him!" She hollered.

"Momma, its O.K." Soothed Ardro. "He didn't mean me. He mean those street guys,—and Momma, I ain't gonna be like them!"

She paused, and taking in what Ardro had just said, she breathed an expectant sigh of relief. "Oh, Honey, What'd you just say? You mean it?

Ardro was silent for a moment. He got really serious. Then, as if he had heard it for the first time, he almost yelled, "I did—I really said, 'I ain't gonna be like them."

". . . Ya. ain't talkin' outta your head, are ya?" She said. It was only half jokingly, because she never expected this, and was thrilled with this turnaround. It was too good to be true.

He smiled weakly, "I ain't talkin' outta my head, Momma." He repeated. My brain's still fuzzy, but I'm really serious.

Helene Beamed. Then declared in all sincerity. "I'm gonna find a way to help you. "Yes I am, Ardro!"

Ardro had woke-up in a brand new day! "I can't be like them guys." He declared. "I know now that I gotta get my act together, and get educated. I hafta go back and learn something about life, and how to make a decent living."

Ecstatically, right then and there, Helene began to make plans. She knew he had good brains, and now she had to help him to use them and get back in school.

"First," she mused, "I'd have to see how to get him a pretty good job for the summer,—Hummn—"

A nurse interrupted her thoughts.

"Ms. Knight, Ardro seems to be doing pretty well now, and the doctor thinks he'll be able to go home this afternoon."

Helene breathed a sigh of relief. "Thank you and thank the lord. This is fantastic news. Now I'm really gonna have to give serious thought to how Ardro and me are gonna to make life better for ourselves"

"I sure hope you can." Smiled the nurse. Ardro overheard this exchange, and sensed Helene's increasing peace.

Suddenly weary from his fight through his narrow escape from destruction, he balled-up his pillow, put his head down on it, and lay there meditating. He felt elated, but worn out. He had had a long hard night, and the morning hadn't been all that easy. Although he was disappointed because his supposed friends had abused him he was happy, because now he had made a really important decision about his life. He relaxed and looked forward to his discharge later that afternoon.

The next morning when he woke up in his own bed at home, he could hear Helene humming her favorite tune. She sounded happy.

"Ardro, she called. You rest up Honey. Here's some breakfast when you're ready. I'm going downtown. I got some business to take care of, and while I'm down there I'm going to see Mr. Mongus."—You know Mr. Mongus, Hugh's daddy.—He might be able to find you a job, doing something down there in his business."

"Oh, you mean the big wheel down on Center Street? He rents and sells houses, don't he?

"Yeah, he's the one I rent from. He might need somebody to help with his places. Paintin' & fixin'—maybe even helpin' in the office. He ought to give a lotta black guys a chance to learn somethin' and make a livin.'"

"Humph," Ardro muttered under his breath. "Don't count on it."

"O.K. Momma, See ya later," he said as he turned over.

Just then, the phone rang. It jarred him, because it was unexpected, but when he picked it up, he heard,—

"Ardro, I heard you were in the hospital. You alright?"

His heart leapt in his chest, and he gasped happily. "Bernetta!"

"Yeah, Ardro, I've been thinkin' about you. Heard you had a run-in with the gang. You O.K. now?"

"Oh, Yeah Bernetta. I'm O.K." Thanks for callin'. I been thinkin' about you too." And—ya know—I'm done with that gang. I'm puttin' 'em down. I'm gonna go back to school as soon as I can." He paused. "Gee, I'd like to talk to you some more Bernetta. I been listenin' to that song I heard at your house."

"It is pretty, ain't it? It's the words. They mean so much to me." She said pensively. She didn't even hear his declaration about changing his friends and going to school.—"It'd be nice to see you again Ardro. C'mon over when you can. Tell Miss Helene Momma says 'Hi'". After chatting about two more minutes Bernetta hung up.

Ardro was euphoric, and at the same time he was uneasy. "Now What?" He thought. "Does she care what I do?" Because he was still exhausted, he continued to lay there, but was unable to go back to sleep. His decision to go back to school got a whole lot of thought that morning. He was of two minds. He really wanted to do it, but he also wanted to earn some money to help Helene. And he didn't know where to start doing either.

"In a way," He thought. "I hope Momma does make some gain with Mr. Mongus. Yeah, Maybe I can work part-time when I go back to school."—"Back to school," he repeated to himself. "I never thought I'd say that again. I hope it ain't too late to straighten up. I almost caved in, but after this scary thing that's happened, I feel like I got to get back on track even if I have to do somethin' extra."

"Uhnnnm"—, he sighed. "I Wish Bernetta'd go back to school with me. Then I could find out if she's really like what Mom says."

* * *

IV

A Mother's Anguish

Helene was charged up. Responding to her new awakening, she started to do her errands downtown. While downtown, the inspiration occurred to her that she'd better catch Mr. Mongus as early in the morning as she could. "He might be in a better mood." She thought. "I'm goin' over there right now."

She headed directly for his office. She strode toward his door, but was stopped by his secretary who said coolly, "There're some people in there now, May I help you?"

"No, I wanna see Mr. Mongus. It's personal."

"What's you name, Ma'am?" She firmly asked. "And I'll see if he can talk to you when he gets through. Please have a seat over there." She pointed to a plush chair in the corner of the small office, and turned back to her desk.

Helene was irritated, and fidgeted as she sat there for a few minutes. Soon she asked. "How much longer is he going to be? I wanna talk to him about my son."

The secretary's eyebrows shot up quizzically, "About your son? And you say it's important?"

"It's important to me," shot back Helene. "I would really like to talk to him".

"Well he should be—." Just then his door swung open and three people, two very well dressed ladies and a young business-looking man casually ambled out, and into the hallway,

Mr. Mongus strode out of his office, and saw Helene sitting in the corner staring after the people.

"Mrs. Knight," he said pompously, "What are you doing here?" "You came to pay up on the rent?"

With a sense of annoyed satisfaction, she said, "I don't owe you no rent, Mr. Mongus. But I got to talk to you." More calmly, she asked, "Can I come in for a couple of minutes?"

"She says it's about her boy," called the secretary.

"What about your boy? Has he done something else?" Mr. Mongus inquired, as he closed the door behind them.

"He ain't done nothin' bad, Mr. Mongus. He's just had a hard time. That's why I'm here. He needs some help."

"What kinda help does he need?"

"He needs a job."

Without a word, Mr. Mongus walked to his chair and sat down with his back to her. Then in a loud harsh voice, he quizzed. "He needs a job?" Why does he need a job Mrs. Knight? "He's supposed to be in school, and I don't hire kids who're supposed to be in school." He said gruffly. He continued. "Of course, I heard about him being with that bunch that pushed that teacher down the steps, but he should be back in school pretty soon." Snappishly, he added, "Even if he's out of school now, I don't have a job for him."

As patiently as she could, Helene answered, "He needs a job, Mr. Mongus, because he needs somebody like you to talk to—to give him some direction. He needs some support. His daddy's not home anymore, and he's only got me, and his street friends, to tell him what to do. He wants to go back to school, but he's scared he can't make it, and without a job, Mr. Mongus, he feels like he ain't got no worth."

Mr. Mongus sat up erect, took a deep breath and spun around to face her. And as if she had never said a word, he prattled on. "His street friends, Uhn!" He grunted sharply. "That's an awful bunch he's messing with. They're nothing but trouble. I don't let my kids associate with them."—.

Helene tried to butt in. "Mr. Mongus, my boy ain't no hoodlum. He's"—

"He's messin' with them though," he raved. "They're a disgrace to the black community. They're bringing it down. Nobody wants 'em around. They ought to put 'em all in jail. The streets aren't safe." "And then they want somebody to do something for them." He snarled.

Helene stood there, stunned by this tirade. She thought, "Ardro's not like that. "Mr. Mongus, All he wants is a job to help him get back in school."

He kept right on. "Ms. Knight, all I care about are my own kids now. They're getting the right upbringing. I see to that! My kids are going to a good college so they can make something out of themselves.—These other kids—I couldn't care less about'em. There's no hope for them."

Almost in tears, she asked as sincerely as she knew how, "Please, Mr. Mongus, but can't you give Ardro a chance? Maybe he can help fix up some of your houses or something. "He can work after school." She suggested.

"I'm not going to trust him doing anything for me as long as he hangs with that crowd. From what I hear, he's like all the rest of them. Tell 'im to go down to one of the fast food places." Callously, he bellowed, "Maybe they'll hire 'im so he can help you pay the rent."

By this time Helene was fuming inside, but, because she didn't want to risk getting evicted next time she came up short on her rent, she did her best to get out of there without clashing with him or saying something nasty. She was near tears as she slunk out his office with a weak

"O.K. Mr. Mongus. Thanks."

What a miserable start for her day! Helene realized that some of what Mr. Mongus was saying was true. "But he's got the wrong attitude about some of these kids. He's not helpin'! And a lotta other people don't do anything to stop it either." She fumed. "He could take at least one or two of them and help teach 'em what they ought to do. As she disconsolately strolled along, "People just don't care!" she fumed.

Deep in her thoughts, she almost bumped into Tina—her church friend as they passed each other.

"Helene! Helene, what'cha doin' down here, Honey?" Tina called to get Helene's attention.

"Oh Good Lord, Tina. I'm sorry." She apologized. "My mind's all wound up." She was relieved to see someone she could talk to, and they strolled on down the street discussing some of the events of the past couple of days.

Although Helene didn't know Tina real well, they liked each other. Whenever she went to church they usually sat together. But they never really had a chance to talk to each other. She began to share with Tina all the stuff about Ardro in the hospital. Tina's sympathetic responses helped her feel better.

Then, as they walked along, Helene slowed down, looked at Tina and said, "Tina, I gotta say somethin'" Half-questioning, She said. "Ya know, Ardro's been love-struck over your girl, don't you?"

"Good Lord! How'd that happen?" Tina exclaimed.

"Well, he came home the other day, all moony-eyed. He was at your house when you came in, wasn't he?"

"Yeah, I remember. The music was playing and they were just talking when I went in. I don't know how long he'd been there, but Bernetta was happy that he was there. He's a nice boy, Helene. I told him to come back sometime."

"Yeah, Tina, Bernetta's a pretty girl, and she was real nice to him. And whatever they was talkin' 'bout, and whatever music they'd been listening to really got him goin', and, Boy! He got the love bug fast."

"Oh My God!" Exclaimed Tina in surprise.

After a short pause, Helene said cautiously, "Tina, Bernetta seems like a real nice girl, but I been hearin' some things, and—" She searched Tina's face.

Tina lively stride shortened, and she let out a deep wail. "Oooh! I knew it. Oh, I knew it! "I just knew some boy was goin' to fall for my child., and she ain't gonna want 'im—no matter how good he is. What am I going to do with her?"

Tina slowed down more. She seemed underneath a heavy weight. She slowly moved over to a nearby bench, sat down and began to cry. "Helene, people are talking about her now. She tries to make out she don't care, but I know she does. A couple of weird girls hang around, and people laugh at 'em. She's friends with 'em, but she's real unhappy. Ardro made her feel good, and she'd really like to have him for a friend, but she's scared of what he's going to do when he finds out".

Helene felt awful. She sensed Tina's misery, but she had to tell the truth. "I'm so sorry Tina, but I already had to tell Ardro what I heard. I could see that he was lovesick right at the jolt. But he's m'boy, Tina, and I couldn't let 'im go head over heels into somethin' wrong for 'im. I'm sorry, but I just couldn't hold it back. And Tina . . . that's what threw him off the track. That's when he ran out and got that dose of something I told you about him getting the other night. You heard about it before, didn't you? It nearly killed 'im."

Tina nodded.

Helene continued. "I know how you must feel about Bernetta, but I gotta worry about Ardro too. Thank God, he's back now."

Tina nodded again. "Oh, I do understand Helene. That's what I'm afraid of for my child"

"That's why I'm downtown now, Tina." Said Helene. "I just went to see Mr. Mongus about a job for 'im, and you know, Tina, that man just about kicked me out. He don't care about our kids. All he wants is our rent!" She exploded.

"Yes." agreed Tina. "'n I heard somethin' uncouth he said about Bernetta too. It's a shame. If it ain't their kids, them folks don't give a damn about nobody else's."

After the two of them vented about Mr. Mongus, they both felt a little better, and they started walking again. Now they didn't care which way they went. They had each other to talk to.

Well", Continued Helene, "you know what?" "Ardro's talkin' about going back to school, and he needs somebody to keep 'im on track. I wish church was interesting for 'im. The church could do a lot for those kids. It would help Bernetta too.

Mention of church set Tina to thinking. "Helene," she exclaimed, "You don't belong to our church, and you always have a good time when you come there. Why don't you join us?"

"I guess it 'cause nobody asked me," said Helene.

"Well, I'm askin' now. Helene, it'd do you a lot of good. Go on down there and talk with Pastor Kirkwood. He'll tell you what you ought to do."

"But Tina, it ain't helpin' you with Bernetta. That church ain't helpin' nobody with their kids. Kids might come to Sunday School. I know they need that, but—but,—"— Helene rattled on, "I wish there was something else there for young kids. I need help with Ardro. Can't the church do something?"

"Yeh, ya'right Helene." Confirmed Tina. "Ya know, all the churches in this neighborhood oughta be doin' somethin' for the kids. God knows! These kids need help!"

Tell you what—, Tonight's prayer meetin' night. They always have a time for testifyin'. Maybe we could testify, and then say somethin' about the kids. We could ask for help to get somethin' done for these kids. Pastor Kirkwood's got 5 kids, and he oughta be interested. Maybe he can help.

There were about ten men and more than thirty women in the congregation when the prayer meeting started. They sang, and prayed, and danced to the Holy Spirit—and they prayed some more. It turned out to be the best prayer meeting Helene had ever been to. She felt truly renewed. Then, came the time for testifying.

She and Tina were exhausted, but soon she was able to stand up and tell how wonderful she felt, she began to let the people know how much she needed the church, and that she hoped to join someday soon.

"Praise the Lord," shouted the preacher.

After an awkward moment, Helene continued. "I been needin' to feel the Holy Spirit for a long time, and I'm glad I came here tonight."

Then, with great passion, she said, "But I also need something else. "I got a boy that I've got to raise, and I ain't got no man to give him the direction he needs. I've got to work to make ends meet. I ain't got a lot of time to help 'im, and he don't have nobody else to help him keep on track. He's good in school, but most of the time he's hated it." She was near tears.

She told how he got into trouble, and got kicked out. "But now" tearfully, she wailed, "He wants to go back, but still there ain't no help! There ain't anybody to talk to except his friends, who're just as left-out of things as he is. They're all getting' into trouble, dropping out of school, and a lot of them are going to jail—all because nobody seems to care."

"Yes." Intoned Pastor Kirkwood, "You're right, Mrs. Knight. Bring 'im to church. We should bring 'em all to church and Sunday School where they can learn about the Bible."

Then, to the whole gathering, he shouted again, "All of y'all ought to bring your kids to Sunday School! They need to learn about the Lord. Maybe that'll keep 'em away from sin in the streets. Bring 'em to church! They'll like the music. It'll make 'em feel good, and then they can go out and face the devil, and shake' im off!

Throughout the audience there were chants of "Amen!"

Mrs. Jones, One of the other long-time members, spoke up. "Ms. Knight. You haven't been comin' to this church long, have you? Well, you know we'll pray for you, Ms. Knight, and help you get right with the Lord. That will help you get through this. He'll help you get your kid through school."

"Turn your problems over to the Lord!" She shouted. "Just believe in Him and he'll see you through!"

There were more, "Amen's!

Helene paused, but persisted. "Yes, yesI know that's true, and I appreciate it. But I'm talking about something more. Why can't our kids come here to talk about school, the problems they have in the street, how to get along with their teachers, their friends, their girlfriends? The church could have somebody here to help 'em with their homework. All that stuff."

The people sat in stunned silence. Then finally somebody spoke up—not so kindly. "What? And have those kids runnin', loose in our church, ruinin' our carpets, breakin' up our dishes and scratchin' up our tables?"

Somebody else chimed in, "Yeah, and the church ain't the place to be talkin' 'bout that worldly stuff. That worldly stuff ain't helpin' 'em get right with the Lord!"

Several other lively comments followed—some for, some against, and some raising more questions. At this point, the meeting had deteriorated from a testimonial service into a near rout.

Pastor Kirkwood forcefully interrupted. "My good friends, let us calm down!" he intoned. "We've all got kids. Ms. Knight has brought up a very important subject. It's a subject that we have to pray about. We have to ask for God's guidance, and I'm sure he'll give us the way to go." Let's give it more thought. We ought to discuss it farther. Maybe we could have another meeting sometime soon."

With that, he closed the meeting with a long prayer—asking that God would save the kids in the street.

"Amen!"

The people filed out—very few of them saying anything to Helene.

Helene's spiritual high had vanished. She was exhausted, and she walked slowly with Tina to the door of the church. She stopped and looked back at the preacher, engaged in vigorous conversation with one of the ladies who opposed.

As they walked home she said, "Well Tina, you told me to tell 'em. I did. Now What?"

"Well, Helene, at least we talked about it. We brought it up, and now only God knows what's going to happen! But I know one thing; I've got to get help with Bernetta—Church or not. And Helene, you get help with Ardro, too. We got to find somebody to help us."

"Yeah, Tina, you know, I used to be all flighty. Didn't know what to do. Always worried about how to please Ardro, and didn't know how to talk to his teachers. "But now," she said with new self-assurance, "After all this, I know I got to do something." They took a few more steps, and then she said, "You know, Tina, God did give me some strength tonight, and I'm going to use it to get somethin' done."

V

A New Beginning

When Helene got home, Ardro was already in bed, but his radio was still on. She could hear the music over his snoring, so she quietly entered his room, turned the radio off, and started out.

"Hi, Momma," Ardro grunted, half awake.

Not surprised to hear him, she paused and asked, "How you feelin', baby? Hope you're feeling better.

"I'm O.K. Momma. Goodnight."

"You get rested now, son." She added sweetly. "Tomorrow we got some things to do."

For the first time since he was six, Ardro heard her say—with feeling, "I love you Ardro." He felt a warm glow as he rolled over and fell into a deep sleep.

He had a good night. He had a dreamless night—without any of the little spells of panic and nervousness he had experienced during the day. He woke up thinking about Helen's last words to him.

He was smiling when he got to the kitchen, and, after his, "Good Morning, Momma," the first words he said, were, "Hey, Momma, can I go down to the school and see My counselor?"

Helene looked up in delight, "Good Morning Ardro, I'm glad to see you lookin' so bright 'n happy. Come on and eat. Son. I've got a good breakfast, and—Yes—," She paused, "We got a lot of talkin' to do. Sit down, Sweetie."

Ardro was very pensive when he sat down. "While you was gone yesterday, Momma, I had some real scary feelings, 'cause I was by myself in the house. I got real nervous. I didn't know what was happnin', but then Momma, all of a sudden it cleared up."

Then thoughtfully, and with intense feeling he said, "Momma, I feel kinda light; Not like that crazy stuff I was goin' through the other night, but like some kinda weight s' been lifted off o'me. I know I been goofin' off, but this mess has made me get the message . . . . "Now," . . . He exalted in relief. "I'm feeling like I just lost some handcuffs!" "I'm glad to be back in the world of people who want to do something. I've really made up my mind now Momma. It's time for me to try to get back in school. I want to go down to the school, ... Today!!

Helene sat there, listening to her son with happy pride and satisfaction. How he seemed to have grown up overnight! In this magical moment, she stopped thinking about all the misery she had gone through to get Ardro to this point. Her determination to find help for him was now rock-solid.

At first she hesitated, but she shared with him her not-so-good experiences of yesterday—going to Mr. Mongus, and to the church last night. Ardro responded, "That's O.K Momma, I'm going back to school anyway. Maybe the church people might help a little along the way. Forget Mr. Mongus. I know I'll find a part time job someplace. Don't worry; I'll help pay the rent. Come on, Let's get ready to go down to the school."

They were walking past Miss Tina's house when Ardro heard music coming from inside. He stopped dead in his tracks. "There's that song again, Momma!" He said it as if it frightened him. He stood still for a few seconds, and listened to, "The End of delight." His mind was in turmoil. He knew Bernetta was inside. He turned to stare pleadingly at Helene. She grabbed his arm, and reluctantly, he walked on with her down the street.

"Ardro, you gotta pull yourself together, she gently admonished.

Unhappily he said, "I know, I know, Momma," Then he softly said, "I just feel so sorry for her. She's such a nice girl."

Ardro had a feeling, but didn't really know, that Bernetta was standing at the window when they stopped in front of her house. She saw them as they approached, and hoped they would stop in, but when she watched them walk heavily away, she went forlornly to her room. She started to call one of her girl friends, but quickly changed her mind, and stretched out across her bed. "Oh, God, I'm so lonely," She moaned.

Ardro walked along—reflecting on all that he and Bernetta had ever said to each other. Most of all, he remembered Bernetta's remark—"You shouldn't quit. You oughta go back"—as being one of the most important things to give him confidence to finish school. It made him feel good. "It's funny," he thought, "everything she said to me was important." Then out loud, he said.

"And you know, Momma, I feel sorry for me! I know I can't have Bernetta, but I wish she'd go back to school too. Maybe we could at least be friends."

"That'd be nice Ardro," said Helene, "but now we have got to get things straight for you"

They were almost at the school when she said, "Now get yourself together."

Mr. Browne, the principal, was in the hall talking to some kids when they walked in.

"Ardro! Mrs. Knight!!" He greeted them warmly. "I'm glad to see you." He inquired, "Have you cleared things up with the officials?" "I hope so," he said sincerely. "We want you to come back as soon as you can."

While walking to the office, Ardro made inquiries about Miss Bundy and Mr. Hendricks, the two teachers he pushed down the stairs. "I'm sorry about that, I didn't mean to hurt anybody."

Mr. Browne nodded in understanding. "Miss Bundy's ankle is almost well now, he reported, but Mr. Hendricks is still in some pain. They're both back. I think you ought to talk to them."

"Oh, I will." Assured Ardro. "I will."

Mr. Browne then directed, "But first, go on up to see Mr. Brevard." Mr. Park's not in his office this week, he's at a counselor's conference. You know where the counseling office is."

In the hall, at the top of the stairs, they waited outside Mr. Brevard's office door until a noisy group discussion came to a close. The students filed out when the bell rang, and they stepped hurriedly into the office to escape the clamor of the hall.

Mr. Brevard smiled at the way they scurried in. He greeted them cordially. "C'mon in Ardro, and Ms. Knight. Good to see you. Mr. Park's not here this week. Maybe I can help you. Please have a seat."

Nervously, Ardro sat for a minute before he happy blurted out. "Mr. Brevard, I wanna come back to school. My probation's over."

Mr. Brevard grinned, and then soberly said, "You were never on probation, Ardro. You were just suspended."

"Uh, yeah, that's what I mean. And now" he said after a deep breath, "I want to get back in school and finish. I want to graduate!"

"I'm very happy to hear that Ardro, and I hope we can help you do that. It's real late in the year now though," and as he leafed though some records, he paused, "and you've missed a lot of time. Humn—, Ardro, I hope you won't have to repeat 11th grade."

"Oh Lordy no!" Shouted Helene. "I hope he can make it up and stay with his class."

"Well, so far, Mrs. Knight, he's missed 21 days this year, and we've only got 24 more to go. Catching up is going to be pretty hard, especially since he hadn't been doing well before."

"Well, Mr. Brevard, Can I get a tutor, or something?" Pleaded Ardro.

"I don't know about that, Ardro, but there's one thing you might do, Ardro. You might consider coming to summer school. You know—it's possible. And if you really apply yourself, you might just make up enough to pass to you right grade next year."

Helene brightened. But as Ardro thought about it, he got restless. "But I wanted to get a job for the summer, because I want to help you, Momma." He complained.

"Ardro, don't you worry 'bout that!" said Helene resolutely. We'll make it. You go to school! No nonsense!

Though agonizing, the decision he made during the short pause was the one he wanted.

"Well—Mr. Brevard, can I come back now? Asked Ardro. "Would that help?"

"Yes, Ardro, I think it might work," said the counselor. "It could make the summer a little bit easier. You may not have to take as many classes."

With a big sigh he said, "Well, I guess that's what I'm gonna do."

Helene Relaxed. "At last," she breathed." I think he's finally turned the corner.

Headed home, they leisurely strolled along, each in their own thoughts. Suddenly Ardro came to a perplexed standstill, and said, "Momma I just had a funny vision."

"Vision! What kinda vision?" asked Helene?

"Momma, I could see myself in a green cap & gown! And then later I see a black cap and gown." And with a faraway look, he said, "ya know, I think there's even another one. Its dark blue."

"Glory Be! Ardro. What a vision!.—And you know? You could be 'em all someday!

"Um humm," he smiled,. "I just might be."

In this reverie, they walked happily back home.

That afternoon they were contented and relaxed. Soon after they got back in the house, Helene began to fix dinner. Ardro turned on his radio, and as he listened, he heard an interesting commercial about a concert down at the Crown Centre. Just as he was thinking that he might want to see the show, the radio program was interrupted with news of a big fire close to Bernetta's house.

"Momma!" He rushed to tell Helene. "There's a big fire down on Miss Tina's street. Can I go down and see if they're O.K.?"

"Oh, Ardro, dinner will be ready soon, but I guess you ought to go check. You be careful Ardro!"

"I'll be careful, Momma. I'll be right back." He promised, as he then dashed out of the house toward the fire.

Everybody was out—Even Bernetta. Without speaking, he stood beside her while they watched the firemen. They watched an ambulance come to take a child away and an anxious mother crying while holding two other small children. The house was nearly destroyed.

The people, who lived there across the street, were friends of Miss Tina's, and she was heartbroken. Ardro followed Bernetta as she went over with Tina to help comfort the mother. As she did so, she turned to Ardro, and asked, "Ardro, can you help?"

Excitedly, he jumped in, and helped move some furniture out of the firemen's way. Then he helped the exhausted family to cross the street, where they sat down on the curb and watched. He sat down to comfort one of the kids.

Bernetta came and sat beside him. He felt exhilarated for two reasons; He had helped some people in need, and Bernetta was sitting beside him!

He began to talk to her. And he told her about what he and Helene had done that day, and what he had decided to do—to go back to school.

She looked at him with soft admiration. "Oh Ardro, that's so nice," she said faintly "I wish—I wish—."

"You wish what?" asked Ardro expectantly.

With tears welling up in her eyes, she said, "Ardro. I really wish I could go back to school with you."

"Wha' d' 'ya mean?" He was really puzzled.

She got up and started to walk toward her house. "Ardro, I can't go back there any longer. I'm too far behind, and I can't face those kids and teachers in school anymore."

"Oh, Bernetta, Don't say that!" He wailed, as he followed her up the street. "If I can do it, you can too!—."

Bernetta moved close to him, kissed him firmly on the cheek, smiled with tears in her eyes, and said, "Oh Ardro, I'm so happy for you." And with a heavy sigh, "I'll be seeing you." And she turned to go into her house.

"Bernetta"—He tried to restrain her—"you can't tell what's going to happen," Ardro yelled after her.

He slowly edged away. "Look,—I gotta go now. I'll be back tomorrow, and maybe we can talk. Momma's got dinner ready, and she's lookin' for me. With confused feelings, he ran all the way back home."

When he turned the corner to his house, he saw a beautiful brand new car parked on the street in front of his house. "Whew, Look at that—a huge Buick Roadmaster convertible!" He said with admiration.

"Wow!" Who could it be?" as he slowed down to examine the car. It sure met his approval. "Must be some big shot, I wonder what they're doin' visitin' us?"

Discreetly he entered the house, and saw to his surprise, a man he hadn't seen since he was six years old. The handsome man, sturdily built and not much taller than Ardro, was dressed in the prettiest suit Ardro had ever laid eyes on. Ardro smiled in recognition, and cautiously approached him. At the same time the man sprung out of his chair and swaggered over to give him a hug. Ardro stiffened, and backed away as he cast an intent look at Helene who was observing the scene. The look on her face was unreadable.

They both were in shock to see Ray Knight, Ardro's father, who had left, ten years ago when all of a sudden, he got hold of some money. Helene had never been sure whether he was running from the law or what. He just disappeared. Until then, the only contact they had had with him was through some court ordered payments to Helene for some of Ardro's necessities.

Cautiously, Ardro spoke. "Uh, Hi Daddy. I hardly knew you. You been gone a long time."

"Yeah, Ardro. Been working. Been busy tryin' to make a livin.'" Said Ray brashly.

Helene cut in with biting sarcasm. "Looks like you been working pretty hard. What'cha been doin"? All them fancy clothes, 'n that fancy car,"

"Well," he admitted, "it ain't been all that good. If it hadda been, I'da been back 'fore now." "But things took a turn. I just had a streak 'a luck lately. Hit the Sweepstakes lottery!

"Well, Whoop-de-doo!" She said mockingly. "I can see ya spent the money all up already; Big Cadillac, Stacy Adams Shoes."

"I didn't spend it all Helene—and it ain't no Cadillac, it's a Buick." He protested.—I brought you and Ardro a little bit. I didn't want Ardro to think I didn't care. Then, he turned to Ardro and said, "I don't want you to forget me, Ardro. I still want to be your daddy," He pleaded.

By this time Helene was seething, but she tried to calm down. "Ray, you want some dinner?

With a swagger, Ray said, "I was plannin' for us to go out to dinner someplace. Come on y'all, get dressed up, and let's go out and show the town what a family looks like."

Ardro could see Helene's fumes as looked at and her, and waited for her to explode. He didn't have to wait long.

"Ray, don't you come here flashin' your fancy shit in our face." She screamed. "We been gittin' along just fine without you for ten years. When you left here, you took what money you had wit' ya—without as much as a 'goodbye'—and all I got was a piddlin' check each month. I've had to work like a dog to help keep Ardro in clothes, shoes, and everything else he needs. And now you—you"—she could hardly contain herself—"come back here all jazzed up, and expect us to give you a chance to show off.—Ray, you must be crazy!"

Ray sat with his head between his knees. There was silence. Ardro looked at him with mixed admiration and pity.

Then—with his head still bowed—Ray spoke. "Oh, Helene, all I want is to let you know I ain' t forgot either of you. I know I ain't been doin' all I ought to, but I been trying." As he straightened up he said, "I think it's time for Ardro and me to git to know each other a little bit better. You know he needs to have a daddy."

With some bitter tenderness, she said, "He's gone all this long without a daddy, Ray. You might be his father, but you sure ain't been no daddy." Then harshly, "And, you know what? He's done real well without you."

Ardro was flabbergasted by this exchange. He was glad to see Ray, but he didn't want to go out and show off. "Just because he has on a Brooks Brothers suit, doesn't make him any good." He thought. "We don't have the clothes to look like him. And then ride in that fancy car? Hah!"

"You don't even know what he's been through," Helene continued, "and from the looks of it, you ain't goin' to be around a whole lot in his life."

Throughout all this Ardro was churning inside. He truly wanted to get to know his father better. But his loyalty to Helene kept him from giving in.

He wasn't sure, but he thought he heard Ray tell Helene that he was going to leave a thousand dollars. When he looked at her, he could see the indecision—"Should I or shouldn't I?"—in her face. He hoped she would.

When she spoke, she was livid with rage. In a very controlled voice, she asked, "Ray, How much money did you win in the lottery?"

"That's none of your business," he snapped. Then looking at Helene's' warlike face, he backed down. "Well—O.K. I guess you got a right to ask. I won $50,000.00."

Without a word, she sat down leadenly in the closest chair. In that split second, all the ten years of abandonment flashed through her mind, and all the anger she felt, and all hurt she felt came to the surface.

"Ray," she roared. She jumped up, and rocketed toward him. "I want you out of this house this second. If you want to give Ardro one thousand dollars, you give it to him—not me! "And Go outside and do it!" She screamed. "Don't you ever come back here again." With rising tempo, she ranted, "You go out and spend all that good money on all that pretty crap to put on your butt, 'n ride in, and ya got a kid here who wants to go to school, and—aaaannnnnd—"Git out. Git OUT!!!" She was breathless.

"If you want to talk to Ardro, and IF he wants to talk to you, do it outside. Goodbye. DON"T COME BACK!!"

When Helene got through with him, Ray felt like a dirty bathroom mop. His Brooks Brothers suit didn't feel good anymore. With tears in his eyes, he tried to approach her.

"Don't you touch me!" she screamed. "GO! Git outta here!"

Ardro followed Ray out of the house, not sure of what to say. Deep down inside, he agreed with Helene, but at the same time, he hated to see Ray so beaten. He had observed other black guys in the neighborhood go through similar scenes, but this was the first time it ever came to his mind that, while it seems that they bring it on themselves, they haven't learned how to control what happens to them. "Man!" he swore to himself, "I'm never gonna let this happen to me"

Then he said to his father, "I'm awful sorry it came off this way." Then looking at Ray as if trying to see inside of him, "I've wondered a lot about where you were, and what you were doing—why you never came home."

Ray didn't even attempt to respond to Ardro's concerns. He just said: "Ardro-Boy, just don't make the mistakes I made. This money I got; it ain't nothin'. Be a man. You make a livin', and take care of your family."

"Here, take this thousand dollars—it's all I got, and use it for your schoolin'. I won't have much more." He breathed a long, heavy sad sigh. "Ardro-Boy, Life is hard. It might look pretty on the outside, but if you ain't got no education it's a real struggle."

Ardro took the money, they embraced warmly, and Ray got into his Convertible and drove away without even looking back.

Ardro stood, and with all kinds of weird emotions, watched that Convertible until it was out of sight. When he moped wearily into the house, he saw Helene standing at the window crying softly. He could tell that she was exhausted.

He went and stood close to her. "Momma," he said quietly, "Come on and sit down." You had a hard day. You're tired,

"I can't sit down now, Honey. You got to eat. I cooked dinner."

"I don't wanna eat now, Momma, I don't feel like it. Let's just go to bed. I'm tired."

"Ardro, The food's cold now, but you got to eat something".

Gloomily, they sat down at the table. Dinner that night was ruined. The roast was overdone, and everything was cold. But they sat there anyway and picked over their food. Neither of them said much more to the other, except Ardro.—

"He gave me the money, but I don't know what to do with it."

"We'll talk about it tomorrow," said Helene, and then, exhausted, they went to bed—each in their own thoughts.

Ardro was soon under the covers, and surprisingly, dropped off to sleep almost as soon as his head hit the pillow. That sound nap didn't last long though. A nervous jolt woke him up, and then he just wearily dozed there, with sporadic gloomy thoughts about all that had happened to him that day. He especially couldn't get this encounter with his long-lost dad out of his mind.

It had never occurred to him before. But the question, "Why is it that so many daddies don't stay with their kids?" wouldn't go away. "Kids need their daddies." He said, almost out loud. It made him recall his friends at school and those in the street. Quite a lot of them didn't have daddies either.

"If they had their daddies," he mused, "maybe they would be better able to put up with teachers, like that Mr. Douglas, whose snotty attitude turned me off to school in the fourth grade." "Maybe their teachers wouldn't push 'em aside. Maybe, just maybe—they wouldn't feel like they ain't needed."

He surprised himself with all these rambling thoughts.

"Only a few of the guys understand school." He saw that often—especially with the boys. "Most of them just quit trying; all of them hate school, or at least they say they do. If they graduate they find a little job, and never go any further. No wonder there ain't no black men teachin'!" he mulled.

The whole state of affairs seemed imponderable—beyond his ability to understand.

"Yeah, no wonder we ain't got no Black men teachin'," he reiterated. "The few black women teachers we have are good—just like Mommas. They try, but the guys don't pay any attention to 'em most of the time."

"I can see now why Daddy 's having a hard time. He didn't do nothin' in school either. Now—Well, I ain't going to be like that, anymore."

His ruminations kept him awake for over an hour. Then, because he was still wide-awake, he turned on his radio to listen to some music. Suddenly, the music stopped. It was interrupted by an eleven o'clock news bulletin.

It tersely stated that several people had been arrested. A "place"—the Orchid Club—had been raided. The police had stormed the place, and the people were in jail. The owners of the place were being held on two charges; one for community nuisance, and the other for the more serious charge of dispensing drugs to minors.

Wide-awake now, he listened. And was stunned to hear, along with the name of Angela Franks, the names of Shad Rick Jackson, and Richard Broom.

"Shad Rick?" He sat straight up, and in a silent yell, "That's Shacky!" He asserted. "And I'll bet you that that guy Ritchie—his real name is Richard!" "And I'm sure the Orchid Club they raided was same Club I was at.—And they got Angie too. Oh, My!

And this brought back that awful night. It started him thinking about his so-called buddies, and his ordeal with the "Yellow Sunshine" stuff. "Humn," he wondered.—

As if this news wasn't shocking enough, and while he was still mulling it over, he heard another news item was even more disturbing. The announcer was more ardent this time. In a different raid at another club in the same neighborhood, the body of a young woman was found in the bathroom after it had the club was closed. There were no details, but it appeared that she had overdosed on some very potent drug.

Ardro thought that was sad, and he wondered what happened. It didn't bother him too much. Although he didn't know who the woman was, he hoped it wasn't anybody he knew, so he turned his radio off, turned over in bed, and fell into a fitful sleep.

His sleep was a mixture of foreboding feelings and images, as well as visions of hope and accomplishment. All these phantoms of his sleep filled the remainder of his restless night. It seemed forever.

Then, it was suddenly shattered by a screaming "Ohhhh, My God!!!!!!" by Helene.

He woke with a start; unsure that what he heard was real or part of his dreams. Then he heard it again, this time it was an intense moan, and a wail of anguish.

He Bolted. Then strangely, not fully understanding why, he sat on the side of his bed, and cried silently, dreading what he was about to hear.

"Ardro," he heard Helene call. "Ardro, are you awake? Put on some clothes and come on out here. There's something you got to hear."

When he opened the door, his dread and his worst fears were confirmed. Ms. Delores, the neighbor, was trying to revive Miss Tina, who was lying there in the middle of the floor. She had fainted. Several other people stood silently by. The look on their stone like faces was unreadable. Then he knew! He had stopped crying, but agonizingly, he felt his last hopes for a real friend drain from his soul. He was empty and devastated. At that moment Bernetta left him.

His eyes met Helene's. Her eyes showed that she expected him to do or say something. But when he just stood frozen, her look changed to one of intense pity. Without a word, he turned, went back into his room and closed the door behind him, trying to shut out that devastating scene from his mind.

He leaned against the door nostalgically recalling, "The End of Delight"—the song he first heard at Bernetta's house. Its haunting melody and lyrics hit him like a Mack Truck. He couldn't stop hearing that song in his head as he bewailed to himself, "I never had a chance to tell her! I never had a chance to tell her!" Even though he knew absolutely that they could not be lovers, he had begun to dream of her as being the big sister he never had. He truly wanted and needed her as a friend between whom all secrets of the soul could be shared.

With all his clothes still on, he pulled the covers of his bed over his head, and drew himself into a tight ball where amid the sobs, the fantasies of his future developed holes in them.

As he lay there, sensations he had never felt before shook his chilly body and numbed mind. He didn't think it would affect him like this. There must have been something very sincere in the budding relationship between them. But he couldn't let his shattered fantasies fall apart.

Instead, to his surprise, they began to take on substance. "Bernetta's encouragement can't be wasted." He suddenly resolved. In agony, he recalled their short conversations; how each time, she had urged him to "be somebody"—to finish school and be successful. Although he didn't have her any longer to "be somebody" for, he knew then, that he had to "be somebody" for himself.

Painful as it was, slowly, and with a peacefulness that amazed him, Ardro began to relax. The hole left in his spirit by Bernetta's leaving him was being filled by the budding plan she had helped him create for his future. Though the plan had not been long in the making, it had taken too many twists and turns, been battered and bruised in its short existence. It could not now be threatened with extinction. At this moment for Helene's sake, for Bernetta's sake and certainly for his own sake he had to pursue it.

It took him several hours to reach this conclusion. When he left his room in the morning, Helene was surprised at his composure.

"Ardro, honey! You must have slept for three hours. You O.K.?"

"I'm fine now, Momma. I'm O.K. I did a lot of thinking. I'm O.K.," he said resolutely. "I'll get over it." But, it's hard to think about what happened to Bernetta.

"You coulda really loved her, couldn't ya?" Observe Helene.

"Yeah, Momma. But I'm so glad you didn't let me get into it too deep. She was able to make me glow but she couldn't help her own self. She was hot cocoa inside a snowball. Now she's all gone. I'll really miss her."

"Oh Ardro. That's so nice to hear you say." Helene hugged him tight.

"How's Miss Tina?" Although he didn't know her well, he had sensed her agony.

Helene, feeling the same thing, answered, "They took her to the hospital for a rest. She worried so much about Bernetta." "I feel so sorry for her. But I guess she'll do all right. God'll look out for her!"

VI

Growing Up

Three days later, Ardro sat tearfully in the back row of Miss Tina's church, through Bernetta's funeral service. Though his sadness was heartbreaking, he only half-listened to the service. He was preoccupied with his thoughts. And in his own dejected way, he prayed a prayer of thanks for the kindness Bernetta had shown him.

"Outside of Momma," he thought, "Bernetta's the only one who ever paid me any attention."

"Now she's gone," he mused distressingly. "She started me thinking that somebody cared about me for ME. Can anybody else to see me the same way?"

His head was buzzing. It seemed that only a short time ago he was a little smart assed underachieving, scheming, time—wasting, and disruptive kid in school. Yet, only a short time ago he felt powerless, alone, scared, unsure of himself, angry, defiant, and hostile. And only a short time ago, he had no goal, no plan for his future, no one—except Helene—that he could trust. Now, since Bernetta's caring had given him hope, his mind had created a vision that all of this would change.

He couldn't sit still. These passionate thoughts were making him restless. Helene grabbed his hand, and held it tight. Meanwhile, his visions of the future made that awful episode in school with the girl on the steps seem a distant memory. That, he recalled, was the incident that had brought his schooling to a screeching halt. He hated to even think about it, and about what happened to the two teachers who intervened.

"In a way though, I'm glad I had that bad experience, he mused, 'cause Bernetta's friendship, what she taught me, and what's happenin' right now in my head, might've never happened". "Now what??"

As he sat there thinking, the prospect that he had only two more weeks before he was to start Summer School both thrilled and frightened him.

He leaned his head over on Helene's shoulder.

"Momma, Can we go over to visit Uncle Berty this weekend?" He later asked. Helene, surprised to hear this question, put her arm around him, and answered. "Yeah, Baby, um hum. Let's talk about it after we get outta here. Be still now, just relax and be still" She comforted.

They mournfully sat through the rest of the service, and then walked home together without saying much. Both were in deep thought, and when they got home Ardro went straight to his room. Helene stayed in the kitchen to prepare something for a light dinner.

Helene's mind was churning. She pondered. "Ardro wants to go see his Uncle. I got to let'im do it; Berty's the only man he really talks to. But Its 56 miles over to his place, and we can't walk no 56 miles. It'll take bus fare, and I ain't got it now. She heaved a sigh. "Somehow, someway, the Lord'll make a way!

At the same time while in his room, Ardro laid across his bed and fought back the terror, and the feeling that his brains were falling apart.

Strangely, he thought it easier to accept Bernetta's death than to accept his own future.

He knew that he had to undo a lot of his past, and that he had a lot of catching up to do, "But will the teachers at school let me? Will I be able to do what I know I can do? "I have to get away to think about it." He mused.

It's kinda scary. I don't want the same thing to happen to me as happened to "Squeaky."

"Squeaky," His friend Lacey Rogers, who the kids at school called this silly name of Squeaky—because his sneakers always made a weird noise when he ran—kept popping up in his head. "I can't get that kid out of my mind." He mulled. "Squeaky was just a regular kid—poor like the rest of us. But his real problem with school was, he's so damn smart that he didn't have to study. Wish I had that problem!"

The teachers at the school kept telling Squeaky's mom that he had bad study habits, and she wouldn't believe it, because "He's got his head in a book all the time." she said.

Up through the 8th grade Squeaky made all A's. And when he got to the 9th grade he asked to take one of the Advanced Placement classes that interested him. He knew he'd learn more there. The school ignored him. When his Mom went to the school to see why he couldn't be placed in classes for the gifted students, they scheduled him for testing, but they never called him.

From then on Squeaky just "tranced out". He just sat there in the classroom doing nothing—because he already knew what they were talking about. He started skipping classes, and hanging out with his anti-"nerd" friends. Finally, in the middle of the 10th grade he dropped out. School simply got too boring for him.

Meanwhile, with nothing else to do, he got involved in a lot of other unsavory things. "The last I heard of him" thought Ardro, "Squeaky was 'pimping'."—managing a house for teen-age prostitutes. Said he was making a lot of money.—

“I don’t want to be like Squeaky. He thought. “I can do the schoolwork. I know I can! I was bored too. But I was dumber than him. I got in trouble at school whenever I got bored. That’s why I’m out here now. And, I sure don’t want to go back there and be bored again.” Sorting these things out were sort of scary for Ardro.

In this mindset, Ardro and Helene both nibbled at the dinner she had fixed. Together, they did their evening chores, and soon went to bed. Neither slept very well—engrossed in their own thoughts.

The next morning Ardro went out into the little side yard to cut the grass, mostly because it needed it, but also in order to get his mind settled. As he puttered around with the mower, he heard the front door, and he looked up to see Helene leaving to go to the store. He started to call after her, but thought better of it, because he needed this time to himself to sort through all the turmoil of his mind. He was still mulling about Squeaky, and about how he, himself, was going to overcome the problems he’d had, and those he feared would crop up.

These reflections were so insistent, that before he realized it, he had finished cutting the yard, and Helene was on her way back in the door.

“Momma,” he called, “did you think about us going to see Uncle Berty?”

“Yeah, Baby, I been thinking about it, bit I ain’t figured out yet how we’re gonna do it.

“Ya know Momma,” Ardro reminded, “I’ve got that school money. We can use some of for bus fare”.

“Lord, Honey, I forgot all about that,” hummed a relieved Helene. “Yeah, Where is it? What did you do with it?”

“I was scared to put it in the bank, Momma, so I’ve still got it in my room. I put it away and almost forgot I had it.

“Praise the Lord,” She sighed. “O.K. C’mon, get yourself dressed, and we’re gonna go right now down to that bank, and open you a account for your money. Then you can take out enough for bus fare for us to over see Uncle Berty.”

Uncle Berty was delighted to know that they were coming. He was the one man in Ardro’s life that cared, and Ardro always had his ear. Though he wasn’t the best influence, he was the best that Ardro had. Helene often worried that Ardro would be as careless about his female relationships as Uncle Berty was, but she wasn’t really too uneasy.

He always coached Ardro to do good in school, because he never did. And he wanted somebody in the family to do it. In fact, one time, when Ardro was in 3rd grade, Uncle Berty sent him a fancy fountain pen because he got four A’s and a B. Ardro never forgot it.

Uncle Berty always seemed to know how to handle people and problems, and though he never got "well-off" he never had to get on welfare. He was always the solid one in the family.

Ardro knew that Uncle Berty had heard about some of the stuff that'd happened to him in the last few months from Helene, but he wanted to talk to him himself, and get some advice he felt he needed from a man he loved and respected.

Helene and Ardro both relaxed and enjoyed the 2-hour bus ride to Hollyville.

Uncle Berty wasn't there, when they arrived at the Hollyville Bus station. They were disappointed. But his son Wilbur, who came to meet them, explained that his daddy had got a sudden rush-call to one the houses he'd fixed up and rented to a young couple. Wilbur left them off to wait at Uncle Berty's house. His own wife and kids were expecting him back home.

Though they were getting kind of hungry, they decided to hold out. "Pretty soon," Helene expected aloud. "He'll be rushin' in here, jokin' 'bout what he wants for dinner."

They didn't wait long. Frighteningly, Uncle Berty dashed into the house in a boiling rage—barely speaking to Helene and Ardro. He was seething about the people he went out to see. He rushed down to his basement, rummaged around in some boxes, and dashed out of the house again, calling over his shoulder, "Y'all just sit still. I'll be right back."

Ardro had never seen Uncle Berty like this. They both sat there in shock. Helene seemed fearful. Something dreadful must have happened to throw him this far off his usual balance.

His truck made terrifying roar as he streaked away toward whatever he was mad at.

"Oh God", yelled Helene, "I hope he don't do nothin' dumb."

Ardro was speechless. This was the last thing he expected of Uncle Berty. "This can't be real," he thought.

They sat there, close together, hoping that Uncle Berty was O.K.

The thought of dinner was long-gone.

Uncle Berty was not O.K. Wilbur soon scurried in with the news that Uncle Berty was in the hospital with a bad knife wound, and about to go to jail.

"Jail!" yelled Helene. "What happened, Wilbur?

"It ain't too serious, Aunty," he answered, "but he does want me to bring you all to the hospital, because he wants to talk to Ardro."

Ardro felt sick to the stomach. "What happened?" He asked Wilbur again.

"Daddy's got to tell ya," answered Wilbur, "I can't. Thank God he's not too bad off, but he might be in big trouble. He feels bad that you have to be here to see this. But maybe it'll be good for ya, Ardro".

Oddly, Ardro didn't feel too worried. Uncle Berty had a cleverness about him that always seemed to keep him out of hot water. Ardro had a feeling that whatever happened would turn out all right, "even if Uncle Berty's hurting right now."

"Momma, come on let's go. I feel like Uncle Berty's going to be O.K. I sure want to see him now, and find out what's happening. Come on, don't worry."

Helene was sort of feeling the same thing. "Berty's always getting' mixed up with some woman. Maybe this was the wrong one," she thought.

"Wilbur, your daddy's a mess! I hope he ain't gone and killed nobody." She said as they walked to the car.

Wilbur didn't say a word, but she could tell he was miffed too.

The first thing Uncle Berty said when they walked into the room was, "Dammit, I sure messed up your day, didn't I? Y'all came all the way down here, and I get in a stupid fight."

"Just hush, Berty," fussed Helene. "You ain't dead, and that's all I care about now."

"You O.K. Uncle Berty? You sure scared me for a while," said Ardro, "'cause I didn't know what happened. I still don't, but I'm glad you're not too bad off, and I can still talk to ya."

Berty took a deep breath, and laid back.

After a long pause, "Ya know," he said, "things happen funny. I'm sure glad you're here Ardro, cause some the stuff I been wantin' to say to you—you saw today. I didn't plan it this way. It just happened."

"What'cha tryin' to say Berty?" chimed in Helene.

"Well what I'm saying is that there's ways to get a point across without doin' a whole lotta talking. Ardro, You just watched me get all laid up here—and maybe in some trouble over something stupid. But there's a lesson I want you to learn from it"

Helene exclaimed, "What in the world you talkin' about, man?"

"Well I'm gonna tell ya. You know I always liked to yak at pretty ladies. I'm never really serious, but it's always been fun. That's one reason Hattie left me. But I got good sense, and I don't get into real trouble—well until today."

"They called me down to their apartment; said it was an emergency. The refrigerator was broke, and the food was spoilin'. I figured I could give it a quick fix, so I hurried on down there."

"When I got there, it was a bigger job than I figured. She was the only one I saw. And I told her that I needed to go find a part. We were just chattin.'"

—He groaned, and turned over painfully. "I know I shouldn'ta sweet talked that girl, but her ol' man overheard me. He didn't like it, 'cause she was sweet talkin' me back, and he came out of the backroom like a wildcat, and said a lottta shit that he shouldn'ta. He ain't even married to that woman!"

"While I was down on my knees looking at the fridge motor, he came over to me, and slammed that refrigerator door on my hand. That did it. I lost my cool. It's a good thing I didn't have my gun, or he'da been dead by now."

"I almost got over it, but then he said, "When you come back here, ya better be ready—Ya filthy gotdam Bastard."

"When I came home I was gittin' ready for 'im, 'cause when you saw me I was lookin' for my gun. I'm glad I didn't find it. Instead, I found the fridge part I needed . . . and like a dummy, I went back."

"Three of his buddies were standin' around when I got back there, and he wanted to show off. I'd cooled down a little and I tried to ignore him, but he started shootin' off his mouth again. And he called me another nasty name. That's when I headed for him, lifted up my fist to hit him, and then felt a sting—just up over my elbow."

"Ya Know? That bonehead SOB stabbed me! **Then—I—did—try—to—kill 'im!"**

It took all three of them guys to pull me offa' him. Pretty soon, the cops came. They called the ambulance, and brought us both to the hospital."

Berty lay there breathing painfully. But he was elated. He struggled to get out what he wanted to say.

"Ardro, He said with awkward disgust, "this is the first time in years that I've lost my cool like that. "I don't want that man's woman, and she don't want me, and he's too dumb to know it."

He tried to laugh. kidding—"You think I wanted show off for you?" Then seriously, he said. "I Musta done it just to show you how stupid it is, to get all ya'self all riled up over somethin' not worth mentionin'."

"But one thing I want you to remember outa this is that you can't let people push you around. That dumb dude's got a real bloody mouth, 'cause he tried me. And now, neither one 'em ain't got no place to stay, 'cause I'm puttin' em out!"

"Ya see Ardro, I got something, and he ain't."

"Let this be a lesson to you, Ardro. Get yourself together, man; I mean get your education, in order to have somethin' worthwhile in life, then be ready to protect it. Don't let **nobody** run over you!

Wide eyed and awed at Uncle Berty, Ardro said, "I guess you mean I gotta fight for what I want, don't you, Uncle Berty?",. "I also gotta fight to protect myself. It's easy to get hurt, but I gotta keep right on goin', Is that what you sayin' Uncle Berty?"

"I guess I coulda said it in a better way, but you got the point, Ardro. Ya' got the point!" He smiled weakly.

Helene sat there, smiling quiet and happy, seeing her two favorite men communicate, but she could tell that Berty was getting drowsy.

Suddenly, a loud stomach growl let her know that Ardro was hungry. She was too. They all giggled a little bit, then she said, "Come on, Honey, let's' go find something to eat, and let Uncle Berty take a nap."

As they ambled down to the little hospital cafeteria, Ardro said, "Momma, ain't it weird that I wanted to come see Uncle Berty now, and this happened?"

"It sure is honey, and it shows that 'The Lord knows best.' How you feel about what's happened?"

"Oh Momma," He said. "I'da never been able to open 'im up like that, and what he said is what I needed most." I ain't glad about what happened to him, but I am glad about what I learned. This trip was what I needed. It's got my head ready to do what I have to."

"I'm still a little scared about going back to school. I know I have to face them teachers. Even though I like the ones I pushed, I still have to listen to the kids about all the stuff that happened. But Uncle Berty's give me the backbone and guts to face it all, and get somewhere. "I used to be scared to get good grades, 'cause I was scared people might say I'm cheatin'. I just don't like people talkin' about me! I'm O.K. about it now, Momma."

Poor Uncle Berty, he's got his own stuff to handle, but I ain't worried. He's gonna do it, too.

By the time Ardro finished this speech, they were sitting at a small corner table. Although they hadn't eaten since morning, they ordered only a sandwich and a drink. Both were too excited, too concerned about Uncle Berty, and too exhausted to do more than chi-chat. Then they moseyed back to the room to wait for Wilbur to pick them up.

Wilbur finally came in. They spent a few minutes more with Uncle Berty, and got ready casually to leave. "See ya' before we leave in the morning." She said."

Helene was still concerned about Berty's welfare when she got into the car. "Wilbur," she asked. "What's this thing about possible jail for Berty, and what 's going to happen to his stuff?"

In his quiet reserved way, Wilber said, "I been talking to the police, and from what they say, that dude deserves what he got. They're holding him for assault with a Deadly Weapon, but daddy will probably get off with paying a small fine and go home. Don't worry. I'll take care of his stuff. He'll be O.K."

"Oh, Good," Helene relaxed.

When they got back to Uncle Berty's house, the lights were on. Helene said, "Humn, somebody in there, Wilbur?"

"Yeah," he answered. "My wife's in there. She came over to make up the beds for ya. She oughta be done by now. Tell her to come on."

They passed a few pleasantries with Nita, Wilbur's wife, as she came out. Wilbur then said, "I'll stop by in the morning to check on ya, Good night".

They went in. and without much more conversation they found their beds, and relieved, slept soundly.

After their gratifying visit with Uncle Berty, Helene and Ardro were ready to face the future. Ardro's suspension had just ended. So on that Monday morning he went to see Mr. Browne, and returned home with an Admit Slip, giving him permission to return to school immediately. He went every day—on time—to school for the final two weeks of the year. He talked to the teachers, got extra assignments, and did the best he could to catch up. Strangely, he now felt more grown-up than the other kids, and he was thankful that they didn't try to distract him. During his enforced vacation, they'd had no idea of what he'd experienced.

Fortunately those two weeks got him back into the swing of things. Less than a week after school was out, and with his future now plotted, Summer School started.

On what seemed like the hottest day of the year, Ardro was sitting in his first day of summer school. In his Algebra II class he looked around at the 14 students there and could see that he was one of only three boys in the class, all three were black. About half the girls were white. Ardro had never attended summer school before. He didn't know what to expect, but he was starting off on a high.

At first he thought, "Well, I guess we're the class dummies. "Everybody else is out there havin' fun for the summer".

"No—He took that back immediately. I ain't gonna think like that" he resolved, almost out loud. "I ain't no dummy! I just gotta catch up so I can pass."

"Uncle Berty sure charged me up when I was there," he remembered. And with a silent vow, "I'm gonna make this summer count. "I gotta be the best one in here."

His other three classes were made up about the same way. On the very first day in his History class one of the girls kept smiling at him. He wanted to, but he couldn't look back—straight at her. She was so pretty it gave him a peculiar feeling—one he'd never experienced before. A couple of days later, she moved to the seat next to him.

"Hi!" He said quietly.

She smiled, but didn't speak, because the teacher, Mrs. Coursin, had started the lesson, but when as she reached over to see something in his book she touched his hand. Involuntarily, he jerked his hand back, and smiled sheepishly.

At the end of the class, she asked, "You shy, Ardro?"

"Nah! Well—yeah. It's just that you're the first girl in school to pay attention to me. I been outa' school for a spell, and it takes a while to get back in the swing of things".

"Yeah, I remember you Ardro. You seem different now. You used to be sort of crazy actin'.

"Now, I'm serious, right?

"Right! And, ya know, Ardro, I like it."

"Well, I'm gonna stay that way now.—Uh,—What's ya name?"

"I'm Liddy, Lydia's my real name, Lydia Dawson."

"That's nice. Liddy's a cute name. I've got a weakness for cute names.

She smiled. "I like Ardro too."

"Why're you here in summer school Liddy"? He had begun to enjoy the conversation.

She sighed, "I hate History. Always have. I just messed around all year; it drove my daddy crazy, and I flunked it. Now I've got to come back and catch up, cause Dad is determined that I go to college".

"Well, Liddy, I want to go to college too," said Ardro. "I didn't take school serious before. I just fooled around too much, and now," He avowed. "I can't goof off any more."

She looked at him earnestly. "Well, I'm glad for you, Ardro. Although you didn't know it, I thought you were pretty cute before, but you were just too crazy. You're still cute. Just stay the way you are."

On her way out the door, she said, good-naturedly, "This is my only class this summer, we'll be in class together, but I'm hoping to see you back in the fall".

"I'll be here—You will," declared Ardro, grinning from ear to ear.

At dinner that night, Helene listened to Ardro's happy prattle with quite pleasure. "School has started out pretty well for him," she thought. Though he looked tired, she gazed at him with pride and a deep feeling of relief. He kept rubbing his eyes,

The words, "It looks like he's gonna finally graduate." kept ringing in her mind.

He casually told her about Liddy—about how they'd become acquainted, and how glad he was that girls found him attractive.

Helene responded coolly, "That's nice Ardro, but Ardro, please don't start messin' around and forget about school." She said all of this, because she didn't want him to think that she would encourage a relationship.

He understood, and then quickly changed the subject to Mr. Bates, his Algebra II teacher. This guy was a friend of Mr. Hendricks, the teacher he had pushed down the stairs in the spring. Ardro felt that Mr., Bates had "kind of an attitude" about that, but he soon realized the fact that the "attitude" was because he had goofed off in Algebra class when he was in it before. And now, he was having a hard time. Uneasily though, he felt that he wasn't getting all the help he needed to make a decent grade. However, he didn't seem to be too worried about the class, or Mr. Bates.

Helene kept noticing that while Ardro was sitting there talking, he kept rubbing his left eye. It was very red. After a while, she examined it, and found that there was a drop of blood in the corner.

"My God, Ardro," she said alarmed, "What happened to your eye? It's bleedin'."

She wanted to know what had caused it. Ardro mumbled something about the math class. She wanted to know more.

He was reluctant to talk about it. "Well Momma, in the Math Class the teacher was talking, and everybody was writing real fast. From behind me, I heard Odell's pencil point break, and I heard a cuss word. I tried to hold back a giggle. I could hear him gruntin' and diggin' in all that crap in his pocket for something—one of them little pencil sharpeners that kids carry around.

The scrunch of that thing sharpening that pencil started gittin' on my nerves, 'cause I was tryin' to hear what Mr. Bates was sayin'. When I finally got the chance, I turned around to see what he was doing, and just then, he put that thing in his mouth to blow shavings out of that sharpener. He did! And by accident, some of that stuff went into my eye.

Helene's mouth flew open. "It really was an accident, Momma." He insisted. "I yapped out, because it hurt, and jumped up to go the bathroom to take care of it.

Mr. Bates saw all this, but he frowned, and said—like he was mad—"That was a bad move, Odell!" Followed by, "Ardro, it's only a minor irritation. Just wait until class is over. Then you can go home."

Helene listened to this tale with concern and mixed emotions.

Ardro continued.

"Pretty soon, it stopped hurtin', Momma, so I went on to History class, and almost forgot about it until now. I walked part of the way home with Liddy."

"Can ya see? Can ya read your lesson tonight?" Asked Helene with alarm. "You know you gotta study."

"Yeah, Momma, I can see, and it don't hurt now, so don't worry. I only got a little bit of reading to do tonight. It'll be all right."

"Well, I got some stuff at the drug store that Ms. Delores said is s'posed to be good for the eyes. When you finish, come out here. I'm gonna put some of it in your eye. It should be better in the morning. If it aint, we're goin to the doctor tomorrow." Declared Helene.

Helene's treatment worked—for the night at least. He ate a hearty breakfast the next morning, and reported, "It feels a lot better now, Momma. It didn't sting and itch and I slept all night without rubbing it."

That's fine Ardro; your eye had me worried last night. It didn't look good at all. Now you be real careful of your eyes today. You're doing so good now, you can't afford to miss school." Jovially, she added, "And you tell that Odell that I said to clean that pencil sharpener some place else."

Ardro made it through his first three of his classes O.K. But near the end of his History class, the burning sensation came back, and his eyes began to water. Liddy watched him briskly shake his head and put his face down on his desk. She wondered if he was crying. She could see that the teacher was watching him too. As she timidly and gently tapped him on the arm, she asked, "Ardro. What's wrong? He didn't say anything out loud. Then the puzzled teacher walked over to him, because she too, thought he was crying.

He raised his head, and tried to look at them, but the light hurt his eyes so much that he had to squint them up real tight and put his head down again.

"Good Lord, he thought, what's happening to me now? This is awful." The tears that were washing his eyes out began to mix with real tears of pain and panic. "How'm I gonna get home?" He silently cried.

Mrs. Coursin was concerned, and she could see that Liddy cared for him.

"Liddy," she suggested, "please walk with him down to the school nurse. I'll come to the office as soon as class was over."

About halfway down the hall, he paused, and leaned back against a locker. Through blurry eyes, he could see Liddy's concern.

"Ardro, is it getting any better?" She asked, as if he were deaf and not blind.

He jumped, because he didn't expect her to talk so loud. "Huh? Uh yeah, I guess so. It's beginning to let up". Her question, and the way she asked it, sort of woke him up. He had been feeling sorry for himself, but now he realized that she was as scared as he was. "She cares about me—really cares", he mused.

The stinging and burning sensation eased up as they continued toward to nurses' office. About halfway there he reached out and took her hand. She squeezed, and almost immediately he forgot about his eyes. He couldn't see, but the pain melted away, as the mixed waters streamed down his face. He didn't care who saw him crying. He was happy!

The nurse had just come in from another school, prepared to go home. But she took one look at Ardro, noticed his inflamed eyes and the tears, and immediately sat him down to examine him. A cursory exam showed that both eyeballs were speckled with fine pencil lead dust, and that the left eye had been cut with a wooden pencil shaving. She bent him over the eye-wash basin where—for five minutes—she flushed his eyes.

Ardro was uncomfortable, but the cool water soothed him, and he remarked, "I hope this helps."

"Take it easy, Ardro. I'm sure it will." Said Liddy, who was sitting there through it all. "I'll call your Mom. Want me to walk part of the way home with you?"

"No Liddy. Thanks. You've been fantastic." After the treatment he advised, "You better go on home. "Your parents are going to wonder where you are if you're late. "Thanks for being with me. It helped me a lot."

At that moment Mrs. Coursin came in. "Ardro, what happened? I was worried about you. How are you doing now?"

He explained to her about what happened in Math class yesterday, and told her, "Mom put some medicine in it last night, but the problem showed up again today. She's probably going to take me to the doctor. I might not be here tomorrow." He explained.

"Well," said Mrs. Coursin sympathetically, "I'm certainly glad that its not too serious, Ardro, and we can work it out if you have to miss a class."

"Oh, by the way, I called your mother, and she is on the way to the school now." Ardro brightened. And as Liddy heard this, she got up to leave. He looked at her, and with the deepest appreciation, said, "Thanks again Liddy!"

With soft eyes and a faint smile she grabbed his hand and squeezed it—long and hard this time, and said as she walked out he door, "Call me, and let me know how you're doing. G'night!"

The next morning Ardro and Helene headed to the doctor's office. On the way, Ardro said, "Ya know Momma, that was pretty nice of Odell to call last night and say he's sorry. I knew he didn't mean it.

Helene nodded. "That was real nice." She said. "He must be a pretty good kid."

And you know Liddy called, too, didn't you? He warily added. "Momma she sure is nice. And she took good care of me yesterday too."

"Mm hmm", she said coolly—and with a half smile—" the teacher told me that your girl friend took you to the office.

"Whoa, Momma, she ain't my girl friend yet" . . . and after a long pause, "Uh, but I'd sure like her to be."

"Umm hmmm." said Helene. That was all

Ardro changed the subject. "Momma that stuff you put in my eyes last night works pretty good. I couldn't read very much, but when I went to sleep, I slept all night. It feels pretty good now, just scratchy."

"I'm glad it helped, Ardro. You sure had me worried last night." She said solemnly, "That's why we're goin' to the doctor now. He's gonna see what that "scratchy" is, and take care of it."

Though she never mentioned it, Helene was worried about paying the doctor—Thanking the Lord, the whole time as she strode along, for the city and social services help with Ardro's other hospital bill. "Now I gotta find money for this." She sighed, keeping her troubles to herself.

Ardro could sense her pensiveness and said, "I'm sorry Momma about all the trouble I'm causin' ya, but I couldn't help it, Momma."

"I know, I know, Honey", she agreed. "It's just that I'm trying to figure out how we're gonna make it. I guess I'll just have to put it in God's hands."

"Hmmm, Mrs. Knight, Looks like you fixed it up already," said the doctor as he examined Ardro's eyes. What did you use? Whatever it was is pretty good.

"I forget the name of it doctor, but I got it down at the drug store."

"Well, it works about as well as anything I would give you. All we need now is to reduce the inflammation. You, and that nurse that flushed his eyes, have done a great job. He doesn't have a thing to worry about now. For a couple of days more he may have some discomfort, but his eyes are O.K. I'm going to flush them out one more time, and you keep using that medicine".

"Ardro, in a short time, you won't even know that this happened. One thing though, you're going to have to wear Sunglasses for a couple of days to reduce light sensitivity during the healing process."

"Sunglasses?" Ardro questioned. "You mean shades? Even inside?"

"Especially inside at school, answered the doctor. Fluorescent light can cause discomfort that will make your eyes to water. And you can't work that way in school."

When Ardro showed up in Mr. Bates' class the next day with the sunglasses, somebody yelled, "Hey Ardro, who you think you are—Ray Charles?—Stevie Wonder?" And there were several giggles. Ardro whirled around to face the joker, and he and Odell both started towards him, but Mr. Bates interrupted, sternly eyed the offender, and then said, "Ardro take off the Sunglasses."

"Mr. Bates, I have to wear 'em. The eye doctor told me to. I gotta wear 'em for at least a couple o' days. The light hurts my eyes.

"Well, O.K." said Mr. Bates. "Just sit down . . . and we'll hear no more about it . . . from anybody." And he went on with the class.

Similar comments and events happened in the other classes that morning, but none were serious until he walked into the History class, where the same agitating Math class dude made another snide remark. "Ardro's tryin' to look like Stevie Wonder! Hey Ardro, how 'bout singin, '*My Cherie Amour,'* he teased."

By this time, Ardro wasn't feeling well. His eyes were hurting. He flashed hot. He glanced toward Mrs. Coursin, who was about to speak to the guy. He knew he shouldn't move. Even though he knew the boy couldn't see his eyes, his glare almost burned a hole through his glasses and Archie's shirt, As if drawn, he started a slow threatening walk toward him This time, Liddy intervened. She bounded out of her seat, stood in front of Ardro, and loudly said, "Mrs. Coursin, Archie's been picking on Ardro all morning." This stopped Ardro in his tracks. He continued to glare, but slowly turned around and went back to his seat.

"Ardro, please sit down." said Mrs. Coursin. And firmly, "In this class there's not going to be any squabbling or teasing. Everybody get your materials out and let's get started." Then sharply she said, "Archie, please stop by my desk on your way out."

Ardro made it through class without much more irritation—neither from his eyes, nor from Archie or anybody else.

After school, as he walked out with Liddy, he said, "Gee Liddy, I'm sure glad you spoke up in class. I was just about to 'bust him one.' Thanks."

She mimicked his almost bragging expression. "You were just about to get expelled again, too. I could tell by the way you looked. And I sure don't want that to happen to you."

"Yeah, thanks again."

He stopped dead still, and said anxiously. "Whoa! I gotta be careful. "Well, maybe I have got too much of Uncle Berty in me."

"Huh? What's that mean?

"Since this girl's so caring, I gotta explain." He thought. Eagerly he described how important his Uncle Berty had been to him, and how he helped straighten him out, and deal with rough times. After hearing about Uncle Berty's last escapade, Liddy understood why Ardro had changed

"Oh, I'd like to meet your Uncle Berty," said Liddy.

He stopped and tenderly looked at Liddy. "You know Liddy," he said. "You really make me feel good. You listen to me. Only one other person ever did that for me. All that makes me so happy. I think about you a whole lot, and I really want to know you better."

Liddy didn't say anything for a long while, then after a deep sigh, she said, "Ardro, I been talking about you to my Mom and Dad. I told them how smart you are, and how you've changed from when I used to see you in school. They know I think you're great, but—"

"But what?" Queried Ardro.

"But they have a hard time with me getting serious about you—or any boy for that matter. "'School comes first.' they say."

"Ummm—Yeah, Ya' know what? My momma says the same thing. She's scared I might mess up" Every time I say something about you, she's pretty cool about it. So I just put it off"

"They're right, Ardro. You know that. You want to finish school. You just told me you're gonna fight for it, 'cause it's so major to you. And I have to go to college—whether I want to or not. So I guess we have to be careful not to get in over our heads."

Dispiritedly, he said, "Yeah that's true, Liddy". "But we gotta see each other." He protested.

"We can, Ardro. We can. Just last night I told my mother how good you are in History, and—guess what!—She said something like, 'Why don't you ask your friend Ardro to help you?' That might mean that you could come over to my house so we could study together."

"Haaaeey! That'd be nice, wouldn't it?"

"Umm Humm! I'll see."

On her way back home from work, Helene bumped into Tina. During their conversation Tina mentioned that she heard about Ardro's eyes through Odell's mother, who told her how sorry Odell was about hurting Ardro. She also mentioned that the Dawson girl is sweet on Ardro. "She stood up to one of the boys in the class about teasing Ardro."

"Are they gittin' serious? Tina asked.

"Well, Tina, Ardro's been trying to tell me about her, but I been shuttin' him up. I guess I ought'n to, but Tina, I don't want 'im to mess up."

"The girl's a real nice girl." Said Tina, and then she added, "You know her momma's the one who works for Mr. Mongus, don't ya?"

"Oh, Good Lord Tina! I didn't know that. Do they know he's my kid? I didn't think they'd have anything to do with Ardro."

"Yes,—if what I hear is right, they know he's your kid. And they seem to like him, Helene, 'cause he's smart and can help their daughter with her lessons."

Helene, remembering clearly the receptionist in Mr. Mongus' office, said with a sneer, "She seemed real snotty to me." In a nicer way she said, "She must not be as bad at home as she is at that office."

"Well from what I hear, Helene, she just puts on that front down at the office. They say the whole family is real nice. They'll probably treat Ardro O.K."

"I sure hope you're right, Tina. It'd be awful if he got in deep with a girl that thinks she's better than him." Helene laments. "He's just getting over Bernetta, and I don't want 'im to get hurt no more."

During this time, the Dawsons had cautiously consented to Ardro visiting for the purpose of study—"especially since he's good in History, and Liddy needs help." Liddy told him about this on their way out of the school. Ardro was so delighted with this turn of events that he impetuously grabbed Liddy up and swung her around right at the school steps in front of all the kids. Together, with all the laughter and teasing, they happily headed toward home.

For the first time, right then and there, he didn't feel shy to ask, "Liddy, can you come by my house with me to meet my Momma?"

"Right now, Ardro? Hmm, It's getting kinda late."

"Yeah Liddy, right now. We got time, and I'll walk you home. I just can't wait for her to meet ya, and to let her know that it's O.K. with your parents for me come over and help ya' with History."

"Well, O.K. Why not? That'd be nice. I can call my mother from your house, can't I?"

"Oh sure," eagerly answered Ardro—not at all certain that his phone was working.

Helene spied them strolling up the street, just as she was going up her porch steps. She stopped and watched with mixed feelings.

"Hmmm," she pondered to herself. "I can see he likes good lookers. She's cute.

"Oh Lord, he bringing her here." she silently wailed. "Why's he bringing her here? I ain't ready to let her see my house. They probably got a fancy house,—and mine? . . . . "Oh well," she sighed; "I guess I gotta get used to it".

She was pleasant in her greeting. "Ardro, honey! Where'd you get this pretty girl? Is this the one you been moony about?"

Ardro chuckled. "Yeah, Momma, this is Liddy."

"Why Hello Liddy. Ardro's been talkin' about you. Now I get a chance to see ya'. Come on in."

She sensed Ardro's tenseness, because she knew that he was going to ask about going over to Liddy's. "Why else would he bring her here?" She thought.

The conversation didn't take long. Helene was surprised that she felt comfortable with the girl, even liked her. She could see Ardro relax. It was apparent that he wanted her to like Liddy.

"Liddy, I think I met your mother down at Mr. Mongus' office. Did I?

"You sure did, Mrs. Knight. She's the receptionist down there.

This is the first that Ardro had heard of this, and with gaping mouth he nervously glanced back and forth between them, as they talked.

"Momma's would like to find another job though." Said Liddy. "She sees too many people embarrassed and hurt, and she don't like that."

Both Ardro and Helene felt relieved, and their expressions brightened.

Then, taking advantage of the cleared air, Ardro said, "Momma, Liddy's having a little problem with History, and I'm good in it. Think it'd be O.K. if I go over to her house to give her a hand sometime?"

She'd just discovered who this girl's parents are, and yes, she's willing—without seeming to be nosey—to accept Ardro's going over to the Dawsons. Of course, she wants to find out more about them. So in order not to sound too eager, she paused.

"Uh Sure, Honey." She said with a grin "I think that would be nice. Now just don't get stuck on it—either one of you."

After a few minutes of chatting, they left.

Ardro happily walked with Liddy to her door. He was just about to turn away when the door opened. He felt a hot-flash mixture of embarrassment and fear, because he was staring into the unreadable face of Mrs. Dawson.

"Uh, Hi," He blurted.

"Hi Mom." Liddy said brightly, smiling at Ardro. "This is Ardro. I know I'm late. That's why he's with me. We walked over to meet his Mom."

"Well, come on in.," said Mrs. Dawson coolly.

Ardro felt itchy. "Uh, Mrs. Dawson, I just wanted to make sure Liddy's safe. That's why I came along."

She glanced at Liddy, and saw her expectant smile, then said more warmly, "Why that's very nice of you Ardro. I 'm glad you came. Liddy has been talking about you. She's told us what a good student you are, and how you've helped her."

"Thanks, Mrs. Dawson."

The chitchat continued for a few minutes. Then, as He began to relax,. he changed the subject. "Ms. Dawson, my Momma says she met you down at Mr. Mongus'. She wasn't very happy that day—but she's nice," he apologized.

Yes, Ardro, I remember your mother. She was doing what a mother does—trying to get help for her child. Although I couldn't show it, I felt sorry for her."

She continued. "I'm looking forward to meeting her. I want her to know that I don't totally agree with Mr. Mongus' about our young men." There are many, like you, who want to have successful lives."

Ardro grinned. The compliment gave him a boost. "Thank you," he said, "I'm going to keep on trying."

"Momma will be real glad to meet you too, Mrs. Dawson."

There was a long pause. Then, he asked uneasily, "Uh, Mrs. Dawson, would it be O.K. if I come over and study with Liddy? I like History, and I might be some help.

"Well, Ardro," she said, "I'd really like to meet your Mother first. Then if she doesn't mind, maybe we might consider some study sessions. I'll call her this evening, and invite her over for a chat tomorrow."

He and Liddy exchanged quizzical glances, but they didn't feel anything threatening about the proposition, because they both knew that Helene would consent. Relieved, he said, "That sounds fine, Mrs. Dawson. Momma will be home after four. I'll tell her you're going to call her."

It took all of his willpower to keep from running. He was beside himself with joy. When he got out of sight around the corner, he dashed home with euphoric leaps and bounds.

Dinner was almost ready when he got back home. He quietly opened the door, and tried to make it to his room before Helene called him. He didn't quite make it.

"Ardroooo! C'mon out and tell me what happened," she chirruped

"O.K. I'm coming." He wasn't ready to show his delight just yet, but he swerved his path from his room to the kitchen.

She got one look at his face, and grinned. "Well?" She prompted.

"Well . . . Momma, Mrs. Dawson wants to see you"

"Huh? For real? What does she want to see me for?"

"Momma! She just wants to meet you." He chuckled. "She remembers when you were at Mr. Mongus' office, and in a funny kinda way she respects you. She's nice, Momma, she really is. She just wants to see if you agree for Liddy and me to study together."

"Of course," he said solemnly, "she don't want us to get serious, or anything. And Liddy says that both of them, especially her Dad, are strong-minded about her going to college."

He didn't say it out loud, but Ardro was beginning to feel a little irritated by everybody trying to put the brakes on their relationship

Over dinner, they continued to talk about Liddy and the Dawsons. For the first time, Ardro felt at ease talking about his social life. He told Helene about Mrs. Dawson's opinion of him and her, and that both parents are agreeable to their kids studying together.

"Well that's flabbergastin'—and I thought she was a "stink-pen"!

"Yep, Momma, She's going to call you this evening, and invite you over for a chat." Jovially he said, "So get ready."

In her head, she was gleefully jumping up and clicking her heels. But to Ardro, she said with a quiet sigh, "Well O.K. Honey, I guess I'll go, if I have to."

Ardro, feeling satisfied with their conversation, started helping her to clean the kitchen.

Then she said nonchalantly, "I wonder what Mr. Dawson is like. Did you see him while you were there?"

"No, Momma." He said, as he started toward his room. "And they never said much about him. I guess you'll meet him when you go over there tomorrow."

"Tomorrow?" She panted.

"Yeah, tomorrow. She's gonna call you tonight, and see if you can come over—tomorrow—Maybe tomorrow morning about eleven. She said that if you can come over, you all could have a chat over coffee before she has to go down to Mr. Mongus's office."

Stunned and flustered, Helene yelped, "Oh M'god! I gotta find somethin' to wear."

Mrs. Dawson met her at the door and escorted her cordially to the breakfast nook. After the first few awkward moments of conversation, Helene was pleasantly impressed,. The time passed quickly, and as they talked, Helene felt the impression that Mrs. Dawson was a strong woman. She admired that in her, and she liked her. They got along marvelously. And they agreed that they both wanted their kids to be happy.

Helene was delighted to hear Mrs. Dawson's comment, "I think Liddy and Ardro will be able to work well together." She was happy that Ardro was considered "good" enough to help Liddy.

This was a good meeting. They chatted for more than an hour together, before parting pleasantly. But on her way home Helene was unable to shake the notion, that there was something Mrs. Dawson really wanted to share but couldn't quite say it. Her past experience of the unhappiness hidden in many families had already alerted her. Mr. Dawson, she assumed was at work, but not once, did Mrs. Dawson say anything specific about him. Helene sensed, however, that he was never far from her mind—that there was some unhappiness. And she seemed stressed out.

Ardro got an earful when he came home from school that day, Helene excitedly told him the full story of their meeting—leaving out only her perceptions about Mrs. Dawson seeming discontented about something.

Then briskly she asked, "Ardro . . . Mr. Dawson, what's he like? You didn't see him at all yesterday?"

"No, Momma, I didn't see him. I told you that." And as he started toward his room, "They never said much about him."

"Humn." Persistently, Helene continued her questions—about Mr. Dawson, about Liddy, about their house. Ardro edged away; cagily answering the questions he knew the answer to. The others he gave a short, "Don't know,"

This left her a little "ticked-off." "Now he's going to start leaving me out again," She thought ruefully.

Helene's questions, though, started Ardro to thinking. True—he had never really seen Mr. Dawson. Only Liddy's comments gave any clue to what kind of guy he was. She never disclosed any sense of warmth or closeness between them. She simply said that he insisted that she must go to college. Ardro too, began to wonder what kind of daddy Mr. Dawson really was.

He had to wait only until the next evening. Long after the dinner hour, he and Liddy were studying together at the dining room table. Suddenly the front door flew open, and Mr. Dawson strode though the hall and into the dinning room with an angry arrogance. Liddy's face showed a flash of alarm, and he saw a real unhappy look in her eyes.

She said simply, "Hi, Daddy . . . . Uhhh, Daddy, this is Ardro. He's—"

"I know who he is," snarled Mr. Dawson, frostily. And without even a nod, he sternly asked. "Where's your mother?" With that, he nearly stomped out of the room.

"I'm right here in the den," called Mrs. Dawson. "We've been waiting for you."

Without another word, he stormed past the den, and headed directly for the basement, followed by a distraught looking Mrs. Dawson

Ardro was stunned. He certainly didn't expect this display of ill manners. He could see that Liddy was unnerved by this occurrence, and near tears with embarrassment. Mr. Dawson was dressed beautifully, but his suit was disheveled. And he appeared slightly unbalanced.

"Oh my!" nervously signed Liddy, "This is the second time. I don't know what's happened to Daddy. He's changed. Last time I thought I smelled liquor on his breath. He's rude to Momma and me, and he won't tell us what's going on."

Ardro was embarrassed too. Feeling like he didn't belong there to see this, he asked, "Do you want me to leave, Liddy?"

"Oh no, please don't go, Ardro. He might not go all the way, if you're here."

"Go all the way?" Bewildered—"What do ya mean?"

"Well," she started with a long sigh, "Last time, he started crying about his job. Ardro, he really cried—just like a baby. That scared me He raved about nobody appreciating what he does. He told us that he didn't feel at ease—even at home with us.

Then he started getting abusive. That's when he yelled at me, and told me that I'm getting out of the house when I'm 18, and he adamantly insisted that I'm going to college. I don't know where that came from, Ardro, I'm really scared . . . . He might not get so mean if you're around, Ardro. Don't go yet." She pleaded.

He moved close to her, and tried to comfort her. After a minute he asked, "What do you think your Mom is doing? Is she going to be O.K.?'

"Yeah, I think so. She can calm him down. Last time, he laid down on the day bed and cried for 10 minutes—all the time moaning, 'Oh, I shouldn't have done it. I shouldn't have let that happen.' Ardro, he won't tell us what's happening at work or anyplace else. He's getting more and more distant. After this fit is over, he might be rude to us for a day or so, but then he'll be O.K—'til the next time. Something's going on Ardro. I wish I knew what!"

Ardro stood there holding Liddy with mixed feelings. It felt good to have her close to him for the first time, but he couldn't enjoy it, because of the family's gloom. He felt that maybe it was good for him to be there, because he could see that feelings of wretchedness and disillusion can come to everybody—whatever the reason. Just then he had a fleeting remembrance of Bernetta, and the fact that he never had a chance to comfort her.

In a few minutes they heard Mrs. Dawson wearily coming up the stairs, and when she came into the room they were sitting down at the table.

"Ardro," she said quietly, "I'm sorry you had to see all this, but I'm glad Liddy had someone here with her." Then, as an afterthought, "I hope you two finished your homework."

They looked at each other. "Yes, Momma," Liddy cut in, "Ardro was a big help. I'm glad he was here too."

To Mrs. Dawson he said, "We did our homework. It was fun."

"Thanks," he said to Liddy.

The next few minutes chat made them all feel better. "Well, if you all are O.K., I have to go home now. See ya' tomorrow. Good night."

On the way home, strange thoughts rocketed through his head. "Damn!" He thought. "Mr. Dawson sure is a cuckoo. Why is he acting the way he is? Poor Liddy and Mrs. Dawson! . . . . And what am I gonna tell Momma? I know she's gonna be askin' googobs o' questions."

When he got home Helene was talking on the telephone. When he saw that she was talking with Miss Tina, he went straight to his room. He didn't take his clothes off, but he laid across his bed in the dark because he knew Helene was going to come in. As he lay there the shock and surprise of Mr. Dawson's behavior overwhelmed him again. Since he didn't even know the man, he wondered why it—whatever it was—affected him the way it did. Time and again, he'd seen that kind of behavior from other men, including his Daddy. He lay there pondering the events of the evening,

Helene's sudden exclamation caused him to listen more closely. He was curious about what made her yelp, but he just turned over and put it out of his mind, because he really didn't feel like talking.

In a few minutes she hesitantly peeped into his door, "Everything go O.K. Ardro?"

"Yeah, Momma." And he said, "Liddy and I finished our studying. It was nice being with her."

"Did you see Mr. Dawson?"

"Um hum. Yeah Momma," he said matter-of-factly, "He came in while I was there. Didn't get a chance to say much to him though. He went straight to the basement."

Ardro knew that she was picking for something, but he was glad that she didn't have much else to say. Her conversation with him was mercifully short.

"Alright, Honey. Glad you had a nice evening. Talk to ya tomorrow. Good night."

After he said good night, he lay on his back and tried to go to sleep. But he was unusually restless. The question, "Why is this image in my head of Mr. Dawson buggin' me?" kept going through his head like a nonstop buzz. "The only thing I know was that, when I first met Liddy, she had told me that her dad has a very responsible job with NCB pharmaceuticals, a respected local company. And just tonight, she said told me that her mother had begun to wonder whether he was going to keep it."

"For all I know he's a nice guy—just upset." He told himself. "He's got a nice home and a beautiful family. They seem to be well off, with a good future."

But as Ardro laid there, some deep-seated elusive emotion concerning this man kept bothering him, and caused him to muse, "Have I seen him before?"

"Nah!" he refuted himself, "That just doesn't fit."

But he continued to mull. "I've seen him before . . . I know I have!—Not all dressed up, and sure not a medical man—but somewhere . . . ?"

On this note he uncomfortably dozed off.

Liddy was quiet and distant the next morning at school. Ardro ached to ask her what had happened after he left, but he did his best not to mention it at all. All he said after class was, "Is it O.K. if I come over tonight?"

"Yes—uh . . . uh no Ardro, Maybe not tonight. Tomorrow night would be good, because Dad says he has something to say to you."

"To Me? About what?" He could feel his ears getting hot.

"I don't know," She said with a half-smile. "He just said, 'Tell Ardro that I want to talk to him.' He wasn't mad or anything.".

Now Ardro was baffled more than ever.

He walked partway home with Liddy after school, neither of them saying much. He just enjoyed being near her, and sensing her need for company. The only reference he made to her Dad was, "How was he feeling this morning?"

"O.K. I guess,"

"Well, how are you feeling this morning?"

"Ardro, I'm scared."

He hugged her as they parted.

On the way home he joined a group of kids going his way, and got interested in what they were talking about. They'd been discussing the death of one of his schoolmates. He'd heard about it in school, but when he joined them, the subject was a big yellow van they had seen on a corner sales lot downtown.

"I don't know why he's tryin' to get rid of it." Said one of the boys. 'There ain't no other one like it—fancy stripes, gold rims, black windows, and huge, Man, HUGE." he emphasized. "And ain't nothin' wrong wid it."

"Well maybe he don't wanna get caught. You know you can't hide nothin' like that. "Yella" Gold, it sure is pretty!

Big Gold Van?? Ardro went into a flashback. He's seen a big gold van several months ago. He saw a man dickering with a salesman over just such a big gold van. It was a strange color gold. "'Yella' gold," he thought then. It's the only big yellow gold van anybody had seen in town. In fact, it was also part of his "dream" just before he went to the hospital that night. It was parked across the street from the place where Shack took him. And as he remembered, the man who he saw buying it was in that club.

"Get caught? Exclaimed Ardro. What was he doing with that van?"

"Man, you stupit." ridiculed one of the guys. "Ya' ain't heard about this new kinda pill you can put in water to make it taste good, and at the same time gives ya' a reeeeeal good feeling?"

"It makes ya' sing!" yelled another. "They call it 'Anthem P'. You can get it at quite a few clubs now. They say the dude that drives that big yella gold van deals it out to all the places."

"So—Who's the Dude, Man?" Ardro asked. Does he live around here?

"Don't nobody really know," said the boy. "Some people say he's a big shot in town, and he wants to git the spotlight off 'a him to somebody else, 'cause he came pretty close to getting caught d'other night."

Ardro didn't say anything else. He just listened to the discussion, but he got more interested by the minute. He didn't even want to think about what this was working up to.

When he got home Helene was waiting for him.

"Hi, Honey, been lookin' for ya'. I want to ask you something."

"Oh, Au!" He thought. "She's picked up somethin' on the phone."

"O.K. Momma. What have you heard?"

"Well, Honey, Miss Tina was tellin' me that some kid—right on the street—just took off, singin' and dancin' like he was crazy, and then ran right in front of a car over on Dale Street, and got killed."

"Oh, Yeah, Momma, the kids on the block are talkin' about Cartrel Morris dyin' under a car. They had just found out. He missed school today. They say he was high on some new stuff I just heard about—that they call Anthem P.

"Ohhhh, Poor Connie!" Moaned Helene. "That's two kids she's lost on the street now."

"Well," he said gloomily, trying to shift the subject a bit, "I guess I ain't gonna do any of that." I'm gonna keep away from it, 'cause they say it'll do almost what happened to me before."

"You make sure you do, boy," Said Helene edgily. "Tina told me that she heard it's made right here in town too, by that big pharmacy company over on the other side'a town."

"And ain't that where Mr. Dawson works? Have you heard him say anything about it?"

Ardro almost dropped his books. Things started clicking in his head. He felt weak.

"Momma, last night was the first time I ever saw Mr. Dawson, and I didn't get a chance to talk him. He came through the room too fast."

He didn't tell Helene what happened at the Dawson house last night, but he had a sense that she was digging for information. He added. And he never said anything about Anthem P."

He wanted time to deal with the heavy chunk he was feeling in his chest. He wanted time to think, and to handle the dark thoughts racing through his head. He wanted to mend the sudden sorrow that shadowed his hopes for Liddy and his future.

"Oh," He silently cried, "I pray to God that what I'm thinking, ain't true."

Then Helene asked the question that shot through him like a red-hot knife. "Does he have a big yella gold van?"

In a flash of defensive anger, he roared, "Momma, why you keep askin' me this stuff? I only been to their house one time. I don't even know the people, except Liddy. I don't know anything about'em. How would I know what kinda car, or van, or truck they drive?"

"Hmmm, struck a chord that time. Something fishy's goin' on," she reflected. Out loud she said, "I don't know, Son, but I think Mrs. Dawson needs a friend. I'm going over there in the morning."

"Whoa! Whoa, hold on Momma." Urged Ardro as it took him a minute to settle down. "Let me tell you this." He took a deep breath. "Don't jump to no conclusions. Whatever Mr. Dawson's into, I know he don't wanna do it. I didn't see him long, but I know he was very upset, Momma. The whole family's upset. Liddy says he even cries sometimes."

"Something's wrong, Momma," "I feel it. I feel sorry for him, but I still don't know what's goin' on. And I sure don't like this talk about him being into the Anthem P thing. Yeah, I guess you're right, they probably do need a friend."

After thinking for a minute, Helene suggested, "Ardro, Maybe you ought'n ta go over there for a while 'til this is all straightened out. I don't want you to get in trouble."

He understood what she was saying, but he just got-in with Liddy, and he just couldn't quit now. "Momma," he pleaded, "didn't we both just say that they need a friend? Liddy needs me. She told me so last night.

Suddenly he gasped. He remembered—almost out loud—"Oh M'God, she said he wants to see me."

"Yep, Momma, I have to go back. I didn't plan to go over there tonight anyway. I'll just call. "But," he said with determination, "I'm sure going tomorrow."

"And you're right, maybe you oughta go too. Momma, Mrs. Dawson could sure use somebody around that won't look down their nose at her if there's a real stinkin' problem. Maybe we can really help, if it ain't too bad."

Thursday morning came after a restless night. Ardro woke up in a haze, when he heard Helene in the bathroom. He turned over for an extra snooze. The next thing he knew she was knocking on his door.

"Ardro, get up, Honey. I want you to go to the store for me. I forgot to get something, and I gotta have it this morning . . . . Please?"

He groggily dragged himself erect. Then she called again.—This time she sounded excited. "Ardro, come here! I want you to look at somethin'. Hurry up!"

With one leg in his pants, he hobbled to her side at the front window. There, she was peering out at a couple of police officers, a strange car and two strange men, right in front of their house. He snatched up his pants, and scurried out to the front porch to get a better look.

There was a lot of loud talk with another strange guy on the sidewalk, and he could overhear the officer ask what they were doing. One guy in the car answered that they had come to town to look at a van that was for sale. They were looking for the lot where it was.

"What kinda Van?"

"A big one. Somebody told us that there's one just like what I want over here, and I came to look at it. They told me it was a pretty kind of gold color. Can you tell me where it is?"

When they described the van, the policemen looked at each other, then one of them said, "I think I know the one you want. C'mon, follow me."

"Wow, Oh boy!" Ardro thought. He hadn't yet mentioned the big gold van to Helene or his strange feelings about it, and Mr. Dawson. "This trip to the store," he thought, "will give me a chance to try to find out if Mr. Dawson really did have something to do with that van."

He rushed back in and got ready in a flash. He didn't see Helene when he came out of his room, so he called "Momma, what do you want from the store?"

"The list with the money's on the table," She answered from the bathroom.

"O.K. I'll be back in a few!" he yelled as he hurried out to do the errand, hoping to see which way the police went.

Around the corner in the middle of the next block, he saw that the police had stopped again, and the stunned guys, following them, were fast approaching cops that were pointing guns at them. The driver floored the throttle, and they "took off like a bat outa hell," thought Ardro. The resulting police chase, and several well-aimed shots, ended in their arrest several blocks away. He was sure now that the van is involved in something shady. But still, he couldn't connect it to Mr. Dawson.

"Jesus!" He exclaimed, "Man . . . this is creepy. I sure hope Mr. Dawson ain't really involved in all this mess. Just as soon as I get a girl—a nice girl like Liddy, all this stuff starts to happen. Wish I knew what to do.

"Oh, Lordy!" He moaned.

When he got back home he hardly ate any breakfast. He felt trapped. He knew he ought to let it alone and let Mr. Dawson alone, but Liddy told him that her daddy was crying. "Somethin's bugging him, he thought. "I just can't let it alone now."

He left out to school much earlier than usual. He wanted to walk the four blocks over past the Dawson' house, but thought better of it. It was much too early. Too risky too—

"Hmm, Why'd I think that?" he mulled. Since He know that Liddy wouldn't be going to school until later, he dallied along—trying not to notice the sickening gasoline and diesel fumes of passing vehicles—just searching the expressions of passing people, wondering what they were thinking about. "Are they as confused as I am?" he thought.

As he sauntered along, trying to clear his mind, he didn't chat much with the kids that strode along beside him on the way to school. He was still focused on the strange van, the police, and the men that just got arrested. Again he asked himself,

"What's the connection? And shockingly, it occurred to him again. "Have I seen Mr. Dawson before last night?" At the same time, he was wondering whether Mr. Dawson really did know anything about it—the van, or the Anthem P. It was all so confusing. "What is he going to say to me, and how am I going to talk to him when he wants to see me?"

"I'm almost afraid to go back over there, 'cause I don't want to know the answers."

With all this on his mind, he was at school before he realized it. He was tired already, and he hadn't studied much last night. In a muddle, he sat in his first class. It was all he could do to hold his head up and keep his eyes open.

"What a way to have to come to school." he thought. I can't let this go on. I've got to shake myself awake."

Thank God, none of his early classes were demanding that day. By shear grit and guts he kept his eyes open, and his mind on what he was supposed to do. But when he got in the History class and his eyes met Liddy's, she looked surprisingly at ease. "Maybe everything's O.K." he dared to think. She even smiled when he sat down at the desk beside her, and she handed him a note, which read, "Missed you coming over last night." He felt a pang of delight in his chest, but strangely, it was accompanied by wary sense of something waiting to happen.

He was really glad when class was over and school was out. Now he'd have the rest of the afternoon to sort things out—he thought.

On their way home, he tried to tell Liddy some of how he was feeling, but he couldn't say it all without telling all he knew. He thought that she was probably feeling the same stuff, but they tried to keep the conversation bright with other things.

As they neared the corner where they parted, he asked Liddy, "Your Mom and Dad O.K.? Did everything go alright, last night?" Liddy dropped her head, and said, "Yes. It was O.K. But it was so quiet, Ardro. Daddy was there, but he didn't say much of anything. He was just quiet. And Momma's nervous, I can tell. I'm worried about 'em . . . Daddy did ask if you were coming over tonight. Are you?"

His heart skipped a beat. He didn't answer her question. "Did he say what he wants to talk to me about?'

Slightly peeved, she said, "No, Ardro. He didn't. I guess you'll just have to wait 'til you get there. You are coming over tonight, aren't you?"

With an anxious, "Yeah." He said, "I'll be there.

The ease he had while with Liddy quickly faded as he strolled toward home, deep in thought. He knew Helene was going to be pickin' at him. And he also knew that he couldn't tell her anything about the other stuff he knew until he'd talked to Mr. Dawson.

"Talk to Mr. Dawson," he suddenly fretted. "I haven't done anything to Liddy, and I don't know anything about what he's doin'.'

"Why me?"—Then—Whoaaao!—It hit him. "Maybe—just maybe—he **has** seen me before." Ardro began to put all of the things together as he walked. The van, the club, the face—now vaguely familiar—the Anthem P, the police, the turmoil at the Dawsons, and the talk in the street; Up to now he had refused to put all the pieces together.

He was dumbfounded that what he was thinking could come so close to his own interests and his budding love for Liddy. "Is this really what this man wants to talk about?" He asked himself again. "Why me? What did I do, or what can I do?"

He was leaning against someone's parked car, and roused himself when the lady opened the door. "Sorry." He said, and walked on, deeply in unanswered thoughts and questions.

When he moseyed through the door, sure enough, Helene was anxiously waiting to hear and to tell. Ardro suspected that her phone line had been hot all day long. He was right. She was ripe with anticipation and questions.

She was in the kitchen. So faking the urge of having to go the bathroom; he rushed through the room with Helene right behind him. She followed him to the bathroom door.

He felt guilty, and she looked disappointed. But almost immediately, she called, "Honey I'll be back in a few minutes. I'm going over to Connie Morris' house now. She's havin' a hard time over her boy Cartel dyin'. I'm gonna help her for a bit.

"O.K. Momma, I'll be here." He answered—relieved, and thankful for the time to think of how to answer her questions.

As soon as Helene left, the telephone rang. Ardro rushed to answer it, and was surprised to hear Liddy's voice. She sounded panicky.

"Ardro," She wailed. "Daddy's in the hospital. I don't know what's wrong with him, but Momma said that she took him in this morning, and when she did, he was shaking like a leaf. He had been crying again. I'm scared, Ardro."

"Momma's scared. Real scared.—You think your mother would come over and talk with her?"

Liddy emphasized, "Momma did say that she liked her a lot, and she doesn't say that about a lot of people." She hadn't given Ardro a chance to say one word. He listened, shocked at what he was hearing—trying to make sense of it. All he could say when she finished was, "Yeh, Liddy, she'll be there. Right now she's over to Cartel's house. Ms. Morris is having a hard time, and some of the ladies are over there with her. But I'll tell her."

Ardro knew right then that he wouldn't get any dinner. But he was thankful at the same time. He knew that after this evening—and without putting him through the mill—most of what Helene had been digging for, she'd find out. Also, though he was really concerned about Mr. Dawson, he was glad that his scary conversation with Helene was postponed.

"He continued the conversation. "Oh Liddy, I'm so sorry. I've been thinking about this whole mess. Hope he didn't have a nervous breakdown or a stroke or something. I got home a few minutes ago, just before Momma left, 'cause I was just driftin' along trying to figure out how all this fits together."

"God! Liddy, I wish this wasn't happenin' to you. I don't want it to hurt you—or anybody in your family. And I sure don't want it to mess up our happiness."

He hadn't told Liddy what he knew about the van, or about what he remembered from his horrific evening the Orchid Club. And he wondered how much she hadn't told him about her dad's pharmaceutical job, and how it's connected to what's being talked about around town. Each had pieces of the puzzle for which they both needed to find the answers.

He tried to comfort her, and ended the conversation with, "Well, I'll be over too when Momma comes. We'll talk."

In about half an hour, Helene came back. Now he was the one with questions. "Momma, were there many people over to Miss Connie's? Were they talking about what happened?

"Oh yeah, Ardro. The place was buzzin' about what happened to Cartel." And she began to tell him. "They're saying that day before yesterday some guy gave Cartel a pill, and then gave him $20.00 to show it some of his buddies and tell them they could buy 'em down at the Fall Lounge. 'cordin' to him, It's supposed to 'make a man outta ya' and give ya' "the kicks."

"Did you ever hear anything about that, Ardro?"

"Yeah, Momma, that's that Anthem P I was tellin' you about."

"Ya' Know, Ardro, They say that stuff's made for people that's already crazy. They use is over at the psych ward at the hospital. It's made right over in the NCB Plant where Mr. Dawson works.

Ardro shook his head. "Wish I knew what's going with him." He complained.

"Momma, Liddy called. She said they took Mr. Dawson to the hospital today. She said he was real upset or something. Mrs. Dawson is home now, and she wants to know if you can go over there with me. She needs somebody."

"But Momma," he cautioned. "She don't need nobody who's going to blab all her business to everybody. I'm finding out now just how private they are.

"Oh, hush your mouth, Boy. Put that outta ya mind. You know I ain't gonna blab real personal stuff."

With an ill-concealed show of pride, she said. "'Course I'll go over there . . . . Like I said last night, she needs me."

A quick hotdog at the corner stand was their dinner on the way over to the Dawsons.

Mrs. Dawson was in the den when they arrived. Liddy hadn't told her that she had invited Helene to come over, but Mrs. Dawson was apparently happy that she came. She graciously invited her in, and immediately, they went back into the den and closed the door, leaving Ardro and Liddy to their homework.

Conversation took the place of homework that night. Ardro and Liddy shared their fears, and their bits and pieces of information. At the end of the evening, though there were still a lot of unanswered questions, they felt much better. While their mothers were still talking, the telephone rang. Liddy started to answer it, but shot Ardro a questioning look when Mrs. Dawson picked up.

In a very few minutes, the mothers strolled together out of the den looking quite peaceful. For Helene, Mr. Dawson's dilemma was no longer the mystery it had been, but he knew she still didn't know it all.

Just before their History class started next morning, Liddy told Ardro, "That call last night was from Dad. He's doing much better." Then she added, "He called again, later . . . . He didn't want anyone else to know it—not even your mother, yet—but he wants to see you at the hospital today.

"What? Perplexed, Ardro wondered out loud, "Why me?—Why at the hospital?—Why today?"

"Ardro, it's important." She pleaded. "I don't know what it is, but I know it's got to be important, because he wants you to keep it a secret."

"Ohhhh, Good God 'a mercy." He groaned.

"Ardro, Please don't get upset now. You've got to go to class."

"Don't worry." She consoled. "He's not mad at you. He just needs your help with something—I'm Sure."

But as a second thought, she added, "Just don't get yourself in trouble."

Nervously, "I sure don't want to." He assured her. "Well anyway, I'll go get it over with."

With a nervous sly grin, he said, "You sure he won't bite my head off?"

And with a heartening glance she said, "He might look mean sometimes, but he's harmless."

The first thing he did when he went in to the classroom was get permission from Mrs. Coursin to be excused fifteen minutes early. He was on edge, and fidgeted the whole time, not really thinking about History. It seemed that the class lasted forever. Finally time came for him to leave. As he left, he patted Liddy on the wrist, and dashed out of the building. Fortunately, he had two dollars lunch money in his pocket, so he was able to ride the bus over to the hospital.

*   *   *

VII

Reality Check

With his heart pounding, he went straight to Mr. Dawson's room. He entered quietly and timidly. Mr. Dawson was nearly asleep. But startled, he sat up so suddenly that he startled Ardro too. There was a nervous mutual recognition. They chuckled, and then they both relaxed.

"So Ardro," he said with feeling, "I finally meet you" Liddy rattles about you all the time. After an awkward pause, he said, "Well, I'm sorry that I shook you up a little the other night. There was a lot on my mind."

"That's O.K., Mr. Dawson. I'm glad to finally meet you too," Ardro said from midway the room. He didn't get closer until Mr. Dawson pointed to the chair by the bedside. When he sat down, he found himself staring into the very face he had seen in the Orchid Club. Though the eyes were red and swollen, he couldn't mistake that face. His heart began to race, and he felt clammy.

"Uh, Mr. Dawson," he said cautiously, "uh—Liddy said you want to talk to me."

Mr. Dawson smiled. That's the first time Ardro had seen that. Then he said gently. "I know what you're thinking Ardro. You **did** see me at that Orchid Club." Ardro stared at him for a few panicky seconds; "Should I run, or should I stay?" He pondered.

But Mr. Dawson continued. "First Ardro, I want to tell you how sorry I am that I couldn't do anything about what happened to you that night. I couldn't stop it."

Ardro's quizzical frown fed Mr. Dawson's story. "I want you to know that I was there—but not for a bad reason. I was doing my job. It tore my heart out to sit there, and in other places like that one, and watch the lives of so many young people get zapped right out of them. I've agonized myself many times over senseless tragedies—tragedies that I have been helpless to prevent." And he began to tear-up again.

"Why'd ya' do it? What happened, Mr. Dawson?" Ardro asked simply—now near tears himself.

Mr. Dawson, with a long deep sigh began to tell his story.

"Well," he said, "Ardro, since I saw what happened to you, and since I feel I can trust you now, I need to tell you what I was really doing."

"Liddy's told you where I work; NCB Pharmaceuticals. But she doesn't know what I do. That is one of the biggest Pharmaceutical companies in the world."

Ardro gave him a sidelong glance. "Are you one of the doctors?"

"No Ardro, I wish I were, said Mr. Dawson . . . . I'm a policeman."

"A policeman!" in shocked surprise.

"Shhhh! Not so loud," cautioned, Mr. Dawson. Nobody's supposed to know that except you and me. **You** and **Me**, ya' understand?

It took Ardro a minute or two to calm down.

"Ummmmm" He groaned.

Then touchingly, Mr. Dawson continued. "I know you're wondering why I'm telling you all this."

"Well "Ya see, Ardro you're the only one who's seen me in both worlds, and can connect me to both". He paused, and then said passionately, "My job is a very important job. I'm an undercover detective, and I'm in charge of protecting the formulas and patents of all the medicines made by my company from theft and misuse. I've got to protect my company's interests, and just as important, I have to protect people from abusing these drugs."

Awed, Ardro looked, at Mr. Dawson. "Oh, Mr. Dawson, I never knew anybody who had that kind of job before.

"Yep. It's a good job, but there's a problem." He took a deep breath. "Now here's the problem,"

"At my company last year, somebody walked out of that office with a very valuable and important formula; the only paper copy that exists. It's worth millions of dollars. Our company created that formula for Psychiatric Hospitals and mental institutions to help people with very deep depression. That medicine has helped bring thousands of people back to sanity, but its misuse by many well people has killed them. It can be dangerous."

Mr. Dawson sat up on the side of the bed; he was very disturbed. He looked a lot smaller than Ardro remembered. He looked weak, and very tired. He paused to get his breath.

"Ardro," he said heavily. "I feel a lot of responsibility that that formula disappeared. In fact, the company has charged me with negligence."

"What?" Exclaimed Ardro.

"Yep, they charged me with negligence." he repeated with remorse. I was to deliver it to the central office, and I had that envelope in my hands. Just before I left I had to go to the bathroom. Not thinking, I laid it down on my computer desk, somewhat hidden by my keyboard. I was only gone a minute. But when I came back the envelope was gone."

"Only a minute, Ardro!" he vehemently repeated. "I shoulda chained that damn paper to me." He wailed. "But it's gone! Somebody picked up a gold mine."

"But that wasn't your fault, Mr. Dawson." calmed Ardro.

"Tell that to them" he sighed moodily. "Besides that, . . . ya see Ardro, I've just recently had my hands on that formula again, and it's got away from me the second time. Wide-eyed, Ardro quietly exclaimed. "Oh Gawd!"

"Now, on top of that," continued Mr. Dawson, "they've just found out that there's a new tainted version of that formula. And it's killing people on the streets. The pressure is on me to find that formula fast. I've got to get it back," He wailed. "If I don't get it back this time they'll fire me for sure."

Ardro sat, almost speechless. He finally managed to say, "My God! Mr. Dawson. I'm so sorry. Boy! You sure got a lot of responsibility, but you're in a real pickle now. I'd like to help, but—right now—what do I do?

"Right now, Ardro, listen—just listen.—Please!"

Laboriously, Mr. Dawson began to tell Ardro the rest of the story. "The night you saw me in that club Ardro, I had been watching two men hovering around that big gold van outside. They were trying the doors, and trying to see if one of their keys fit it. I didn't know it then, but they managed to get inside. Then, I saw them strolling about in that room.

"Yeah, I remember seeing that van in the lot. Was it theirs?"

"Nope, it wasn't theirs. But Ardro, they managed to get into that van."

"Uhn? Then I wonder what they were doing in it."

"Hold still, Ardro. I'm coming to that."

Mr. Dawson continued. "I was in that place for an hour and a half, and watched them sell a whole package of pills—two or three at a time—to the people that ran the place. I don't know whether those pills came NCB or not."

"And Ardro," There was a long pause, "I still shudder when I think about it." With his head lowered in disgusted deliberation, he said, "I also saw that woman put that 'acid' in your drink. Ardro, even though I didn't know you then, I almost cried that night too, when I heard about what happened to you."

He got real quiet, and then went on with his story. "Anyway, I was pretty sure that they stole—or knew who stole—our formula—.

Soon after you left, I went over to them, and struck up a conversation, to see what I could find out. We just chatted. I watched them make another deal, then, pretty soon they decided to leave"

"I musta' looked like a pretty cool zubber," he grinned, "they let me bum a ride with them to another club"

"I had to ride in the backseat. I'd never been back there before, and it felt kind of funny." Ardro frowned, and thought, "Before??" . . . But Mr. Dawson kept on going. "When I sat down I heard paper crumple—an unusual sound in a seat. "—And Ardro, just under that seat, I felt an envelope—not just any envelope—but my envelope; an NCB envelope. I'd know it anywhere. Its texture is different from any other. It was stuck under the springs in that seat."

"I sat there for two whole blocks, making small-talk, trying to figure out what to do. Then I eased my little gun out of my jacket and waited.

"At the next red traffic light I jumped up, fired a blank round and screamed, 'Stop! You're under arrest.' It petrified 'em. They were so scared they were real bullets that they almost puked, they gave up right away."

Mr. Dawson chuckled, and Ardro laughed out loud, as they visualized the scene. "Just then, "He said, "The city police came and arrested the guys for selling drugs"

At that point, he became very serious. The details were what he wanted Ardro to understand.

"The police," he explained, "didn't know what I was after. They just thought it was one of my regular drug busts. So before I could get back into the van and recover the NCB envelope, one of them drove that van away."

"They moved too fast." He said with exasperation, after a couple of seconds to settle down. "I latter found out that they took the van back to my company's main office. "Ardro, ya see,." he continued, "I didn't tell you this. That's a company van. That's the one I was using for my undercover work. That's why they took it back to the company." And then before I knew it, it was up for sale."

Ardro's mouth flew open.

Agitated, Mr. Dawson continued. "Ardro, I'm absolutely sure that envelope had the formula in it." He yelped. "There's no other envelope like it on the street." With a loud moan, "—But I left it in the van!"

I didn't know it then, but now I know that they'd stashed something in it. I just figured then, that they were the ones I'd have to watch. That's the reason I was there inside that club."

"Oh Lord!" Exhausted, Mr. Dawson lay back down. "And now Ardro, I'm in deep trouble at work," He lamented. "I've lost the formula again."

Wretchedly, and with a heavy sigh, he continued. "I know I should have been more careful. I just couldn't tell those cops everything; I didn't want to get arrested too, so I just wasn't quick enough.

"For that reason now, if that formula and any other stuff is still in that van, and if it's found by the company, they're sure to think that I'm the one who stole it in the first place." He continued, now in a shaky voice,. "But even if I can convince them that I didn't steal it, I sure can't tell them that I let it get away from me the second time."

Mr. Dawson looked pleadingly at Ardro. "I know you must feel helpless, but Ardro, I need your help. My family needs your help."

"I can't loose my job over a careless mistake." He cried. "You're the only person in the world I can ask."

Ardro pulled his chair up close to the bed. Stunned and confused, he asked earnestly, "What can **I** do, Mr. Dawson? I don't know what to do. They looked agonizingly at each other, and he and put his head down on the bed. Now it was his turn to cry, and Mr. Dawson patted him gently.

After a long silence, “You know where that van is, Ardro?” asked Mr. Dawson abruptly.

Ardro sat up straight. “Uhn, no, Not exactly, Mr. Dawson. He said slowly. The boys on the street say they saw it in a sales lot downtown.”

Then, with a flinch, “Ooooh, Mr. Dawson, you don’t want me to get in it, do ya?” He asked, alarmed. “The cops arrested some shady looking dudes yesterday because they came to town to buy it. That’d be real tricky”

Mr. Dawson looked Ardro straight in the eye, and said. “Tricky is what we’ve got to be in this business.”

Ardro shuddered. “This is scary . . . and . . . and strange, and so new, Mr. Dawson. But because of Liddy, and what you’re trying to do is good for our neighborhood. I guess the only thing I can say is,—I wanna try to help.—

After a long pause, “Yeah, Mr. Dawson,” he said resolutely, “Just tell me what has to be done, and how to do it . . . . “And, I’ll try my best to do it.”

On the way home from his hospital visit with Mr. Dawson, the bus seemed to crawl. Ardro knew that Helene was expecting him at least half an hour ago. She didn’t even know that he had gone to visit Mr. Dawson, and she’d be full of questions. He was glad, though, that he had a seat by himself, and that he didn’t have to talk to anybody. It gave him a chance to think through Mr. Dawson’s scheme. His phrase, “Tricky, is what we’ll have to be.” kept ringing in his ears. He couldn’t waver now. He knew he had to do it. So he’d have to learn the tricks.

“Well,” he heaved a sigh. “I gotta grow up sometime. “I’m gonna do it; at least I’m gonna give it a try.”

He got off the bus and hurried home. Helene was waiting.

“You and Liddy, took the long way home.” Said Helene, with a question in her voice. He knew she wanted him to explain his lateness, but he simply said. “No Momma, I had some other things to do. Tell ya’ about it later. Uh,—Momma—he excused himself—I have to get some studying done now, ’cause I want to go over and help Liddy for a while.” And he rushed off to his room.

Disappointed, she shook her head. “He knows more than he’s tellin’ me, and he’s shuttin’ me out again.” she thought. “But I’ll get’im at dinner.

Even that hope was dashed for he when he came out of the bathroom a few minutes later, and announced, “Momma, Liddy asked me to come over to have dinner with them before we study. That O.K?”

“Yeah, Honey,” she said. And brightly, hiding her let-down feeling, “that’ll just save me from cookin’.” Yet, she couldn’t hide from herself her feelings of dejection and puzzlement as she watched him go back into his room.

In his room Ardro tried—he really tried—to get his mind on his homework, He kept thinking about what lie before him. Mr. Dawson's plan—"Go down there and act like you want to buy that van."—kept drifting back to his head. He wanted to think it through. "Don't I look too young for that?" He had asked.

Now, he was considering what Mr. Dawson had said, "Ardro, you know guys younger than you who are doing that. They go down there with plenty of money in their pockets. Nobody knows where they get it, and they buy anything they want. All, those salespeople want is your money, and they don't care where it comes from."

"Hmnn. Yeah, he's right." he thought. "I guess I could act like I know what I'm doin'. All I have to do is make'em think I got a lotta money."

Fortunately, his homework for that night didn't take too much concentration, because is mind was fully preoccupied with the problems facing him about what he had agreed to do for Mr. Dawson.

He paced his bedroom floor. Asking himself, "Now I gotta find out where that van is . . . . And there're other problems I got to solve How am I going to get inside that van without that salesman taggin' along?."

He realized with dread, that he'd have to search the van unnoticed, and find out if, in fact the, envelope was still there. Mr. Dawson had already told him that the cops—or even worse, the company—might have recovered it. He had also asked him to check that any other stuff, like drugs or papers, might have been planted in there. "Get them out, too, if you can."

"Gettin, in, findin' the stuff and getting' out is goin' to be real tricky." He fretted" I ain't gonna have no coat on, cause it's hot outside now. I gotta figure out how to hide whatever I find."

For over fifteen minutes, his head rattled with these considerations. His mind wouldn't stay on his math. Ardro was scared, but he was excited.

It occurred to him then, that undercover work was something he'd never thought about before. It fascinated him. At the time, his only thoughts were of such dangers as getting shot or getting caught. The dangers of his own temptation and greed never entered his mind.

Suddenly he felt lonely. Nobody knew what he knew, and he couldn't tell anybody anything—not even Helene or Liddy.

He lifted his head from his desk, and realized that he'd been asleep for at least 10 minutes. "Damn," he swore as he looked at his paper—his math scribbles impossible to read. "It's almost supper time, and I haven't done a thing. I've got to keep my head together. I can't let school slide."

Just then he heard. "Ardro, You still goin' out? It's gettin' late."

He really didn't want to, but he went to the kitchen, and sat down heavily. "Yeah, Momma, I'm going. But before I go" . . . . He stopped and looked at her lovingly—"I wanna tell you Momma, that I'm sorry I couldn't talk to you when I came home. He chose his words carefully.

"You know, Momma—this gossip about Mr. Dawson, and about Cartel dying, and kids on the street gittin' that stuff—it's got Liddy and everybody else all upset. And it's got me so upset I can't do my work." It's hard for me to concentrate.

"Oh. Lord, Ardro, Don't let that happen," moaned Helene. "Ya can't let nothin' stop you now."

"I won't. Momma, but I sure wanna get through this"

"But now," He sighed, "I gotta go, Momma." And as he turned to leave, he explained further—I've been trying to help Mr. Dawson. He's sick and in trouble, not because he's dealing, but it's because he's not. I can't tell you anymore now, 'cause I gotta go."

"Liddy and I can help each other, and we have work to do. Dinner's about ready over there anyway."

He quickly left, leaving Helene sort of breathless. And feeling rather uneasy, she silently vowed, "I'm going over there tomorrow."

Dinner with the Dawsons was awkward. The food—not as satisfying and filling as Helene's—was good. Nobody said much about Mr. Dawson, but it was plain that they all were thinking about him and all the hubbub in the community.

Mrs. Dawson left them and went to the kitchen when she finished her dinner, and then quietly to the living room to do some reading. Within a half-hour she returned to the dining room with a quiet thoughtful smile, musingly interrupting their conversation and study. They looked really somber, and she knew that not much study had been going on. She hated to see them so worried.

"Ardro," she began slowly, "again I'm sorry that Mr. Dawson was rude to you the other night when came in. He was so upset, Ardro. He's not normally that way." She dabbed at her eyes because tears began to show.

Her tears troubled him, and he felt awkward. "That's O.K. Mrs. Dawson, I wasn't offended, just surprised." he said hesitantly.

"Well, he's sorry too." she continued. "He really admires you now, Ardro, because he thinks you're an intelligent young man. He told me that you made him feel better when you came to see him today. And he was surprised that you were so easy to talk to and so quick to understand his problem."

She stepped closer, and laid her hand on his. "And Now, Ardro, He's depending on you. He says you're the only person in the world who can help him. Something happened on his job that he feels terribly responsible for—a mistake that could cost thousands of lives. I don't know all the details, but I do know he sure trusts you. Right now you're a pretty important person to him, Ardro."

She paused for a long moment.

Then Liddy joined in. "Ardro, I'm glad that Daddy likes you. I sure hope you can help him without it causing you any trouble."

Mrs. Dawson continued. "He's so secretive about his job, Ardro. He won't tell us all that's happened, but I'm glad he talked with you, because I know that whatever is going on, is causing him pain, and he needs help. I just had to tell you this, Ardro, because we'll appreciate everything you do to help him."

"Thanks, Mrs. Dawson," He said carefully, "Whatever I do is because I think a lot of Liddy and you. Just thinking about what it is, is awesome."

This conversation brought to mind Helene and the anxiety she must be feeling—especially since she been uninformed about how he's fitting into all the turmoil of the Dawson family and the unrest in community. So he spoke up. "Uh, Mrs. Dawson, Momma's been hearing a whole lot of gossip from her friends. She's been trying to pick me for information, but I can't tell her all I know. Since she met you, she likes you and sorta knows what you're going through. Maybe you could help her to understand. She'll be back over. That O.K?"

"That would be really nice, Ardro." She said, vibrantly. "Maybe we can help each other. Tell her to come on over anytime."

"Momma's kinda nosey, but she's nice. She really wants to help. I'll tell her. But . . . when she comes over, would you please explain to her that Mr. Dawson asked me not to tell everything. Just let her know that I'm not doing anything wrong or illegal, but please tell her not to ask too many questions."

"Yes, of course, I'll be glad to do that" Said Mrs. Dawson as she slowly left the room.

Soon after that, he and Liddy ended the evening with a quiet embrace.

Although he had more homework to do, Ardro didn't feel the need to hurry home. He leisurely strolled along, feeling a strange tightness in his shoulders.

"I gotta think of how I'm gonna get that stuff for Mr. Dawson," he mused. Then he thought, "Man I can't let all this stuff bring me off my track. I got school!" That thought was quickly given momentum by the excitement of doing undercover work. "Humn, it might be fun to be a G-Man or somethin' exciting like that for a living." He mulled.

His mind was full of conflicting thoughts and feelings. He wanted desperately for all the confusion to go away, and be replaced with just freedom to court Liddy and go to school. "I'll get through it." He told himself.

A half hour later than usual, he strode through the front door. Helene appeared to be dozing, but he could tell that she was waiting for him to begin his report of the evening.

He didn't give her a chance to ask anything, and after they exchanged greetings, he abruptly stated, "Momma, after school tomorrow, I'd like to go downtown.

"For what?" She asked.

Well Momma, there's a job I have to do downtown for Mr. Dawson on one of the car lots. I've got to go look at something. Maybe I can get some information he needs out of it. I hope so".

He spoke so fast and jumbled that she looked at him with concern. "I don't know what you're talkin' about, Ardro," Helene said. "I been hearing about all this stuff, and that maybe Mr. Dawson's mixed up in it. Can't ya tell me nothing, Ardro?"

"Momma I know you're worried about me, but all I can say now"—and he spoke very deliberately—"is that I am not doing anything bad. All I'm doing is helping out the Dawson family. They're nice people, Momma, and I really like Liddy. I'm doing it for them. I can't tell you all the details now, because it's about Mr. Dawson's job."

"Mrs. Dawson, saying anything about it?" Asked Helene pointedly.

"Yeah, Momma," he said thoughtfully. And she's very upset, 'cause she don't know a whole lot either. But she's happy I'm going to try to help him. And Momma, she said that maybe you and her could help each other."

"She said that?"

"Yep, and she said It'd be real nice if you'd come over, so you two could talk."

Helene, now mollified, agreed. "Humn, well, I guess I could run over there tomorrow to see if there's anything I can do. And, if whatever you do is gonna help Mr. Dawson, I guess its O.K."

Then after a long pause, Ardro piped up. "Uh . . . Momma, I'm gonna need to borrow your big gold chain—the one with the big cross on it."

"Huh?"

"Yeah," He grinned broadly, "I'm gonna dress up like a ol' lady after school tomorrow"

"Gid outa here!! No you ain't! Giggled Helene.

The big belly-laugh melted the tension. Ardro then said, "No, Momma, Its just that I hafta look like I got money. You know, those guys wear all this gold and stuff. When I go down to this car lot, I gotta look like that."

"Tryin' to follow your Daddy's footsteps," she said sarcastically.

That remark hurt . . . . Ardro fell silent, then said pitifully, "Don't say that, Momma."

"Oh O.K, Baby, I know." She said gently. "I know you got a tricky job to do, and you'll do it too, I know you will! Just be careful, Baby, be careful." And she hugged him tightly.

"There's that word 'tricky' again." He thought. And excitement began to replace the worry, as he headed to his bedroom. He was glad that all his school tests were over so that he could spend the rest of the evening getting his head together for his risky escapade.

He was tired, but he was keyed up too. For the first time ever, he found himself thinking carefully about what he was going to wear for an occasion. He lay across his bed picturing himself as he hoped he would look tomorrow at the car lot. "I don't want to look like a rich thug; I just want to look cool, rich and businesslike.—And a little bit older." he thought.

His lean tight body, he knew, would look good in his best jet-black tee shirt, and his slim black jeans. "Damn," He exclaimed silently. "I got to wear all that black stuff on the hottest day of the year." He shrugged his shoulders. "But that's the breaks."

"Momma's big gold chain and cross will look pretty cool too, and—uhmmm, I hope one of her gold colored rings will fit me. Maybe they'll think I'm old enough to be married "He planned to top off his get-up with a black attaché case, which he borrowed from Mrs. Dawson.

After all that planning, he carefully rehearsed the story he carefully trumped up for his transaction at the car lot.

Although he was tired, he thought he wouldn't be able to sleep well that night, but Friday morning came quickly, and he woke up refreshed and energized. At school he and Liddy both felt more relaxed than they had felt for several days.

When he went home after school to change clothes, Helene wasn't there. He was disappointed, because he hadn't asked her about the ring. But she had surprised him. Thoughtfully, she had put exactly the ring he had hoped for, on his dresser alongside the gold chain and cross. "Oh, Momma, Bless you," he thought.

In that moment, that chain, that cross and that ring looked more beautiful than he had ever seen them before. They shined with the love and support of his mother. With a glance of approval in the mirror, he started on his mission.

The young salesman looked up from his desk as Ardro approached. He was surprised to see a guy, who seemed even younger than he, looking so casually businesslike.

As Ardro walked in, he spoke first; without giving the salesman a chance to speak. "Uh, I've been seeing that old van on the back of your lot for a couple of weeks. It's for sale isn't it?" He tried to sound adult and experienced.

"Yes Sir, it sure is. And in good running shape too. Would you like to look at it?"

"Well," He tried to sound important. "You see, I work for a church group that's in need of a van. That one looks kind of fancy, but maybe if the price is right, it might do. We could get it painted." He hedged.

"Hmm, Yes, I think we could give you a good deal on it, Sir. As you say, its been sittin' there for a while, and—yes, some other church groups have been asking about it too, but when they found out it used to belong to a drug runner they left in a hurry.

"Drug runner! He quizzed in mock concern. "Well, that ought'a knock the price down a whole lot," chuckled Ardro. "What's it like inside?"

"Would you like to check it out?"

"Well, He appeared to be uncertain . . . Humn, since it's got a shady reputation—he emphasized 'shady'—I'd better give it a good inspection—inside and out, don't ya think? Yes, I think I'd like to check it out. We wouldn't want any surprises, now would we?" He chuckled.

The salesman hesitated. "Uh,—but there's one little problem. It's locked."

"Don't you have a key?"

"Yes we do, but—the salesman said cautiously—the police want us to be very careful about who we let to inside that van. I don't know why, but there's something about it that's tricky."

"Tricky? What's tricky? Now I see why people run." He bristled. "Anyway, all I want to do is look around in the inside, and be able to tell the ladies in the church group what it looks like."

"They're sure to want to come down and see for themselves before they buy. And I think if you can give the church a good deal, we might be able to pay cash."

"Cash!" The salesman brightened. "Yes Sir! In that case I think we might be able to give you a real good deal."

"But I'll have to see inside first." Persisted Ardro. "I know they'll want me to inspect it to be sure it's clean."

"You said you'd be willing to pay cash?"

"Why sure," said Ardro, deadpan. "If the price is right, and it suits the church's needs."

"Well, O.K." He said resignedly, I guess it's all right." He guardedly handed over the key, as he said, "It's hot in there, so I know you won't be staying long. I'll wait for you out here."

"Boy that went well," thought Ardro as he gratefully strolled toward the van. He took a deep breath before he entered the stifling van, and hurriedly set about searching for that most important envelope. The mixture of heat, body odor and some other strange smell made him feel a bit queasy.

In a while, his heart thumped with excitement as he reached under the seats, where the springs were so hot that he thought the paper might be burned. But after what seemed like forever, he finally touched an envelope, which almost fell into his hands. He was wringing wet with sweat from the heat and the excitement. It had taken him only a couple of never-ending minutes to make this find. But disappointingly, inside that envelope were several packets of a substance he'd never seen before. The formula wasn't there. Frustrated, he quickly stuffed it into his attaché case snapped it shut and stepped outside to gasp some cooler air.

He waved at the salesman who was watching him from the office door. "Had to come up for air," he yelled. "One more time.—I'm almost finished looking."

After a minute, he reentered the sweltering van, and went directly to the rear. Under the springs of that seat he renewed his search for the formula. Then as he sat on the seat in front of it, he heard—what Mr. Dawson must have heard—the peculiar crinkling sound of paper. And with a slight tug, he pulled out a smaller than expected envelope that had a unique tough leathery texture. It felt strange.

"Yeah! This is it!" he exalted. With his heart pounding, he put it in the attaché case, just as he heard someone approach the van. He was backing toward the door when the salesman asked, "Well what do you think, Sir?"

"Well, lemme get outa here to a cooler spot first, and I can tell ya," Said Ardro, breathing heavily. "Whew! I sure hope the air conditioner works in this thing, because whoever buys it is sure going to need it."

"Oh, Yes Sir." The guy assured him, "the air works just fine. Had it checked just the other day . . . . Well, what do you think?"

As they walked back towards the office, Ardro tried to speak with some authority. "Well," he said. "It's in pretty good shape, but kind of fancy for church folks—you know—big seats 'n everything. It won't hold too many. I think it's clean of 'you-know-what'. But it's got a strange odor. Maybe if you air it out a bit it'll be O.K.

"Oh, It'll be aired out, and nice and clean too" Assured the salesman.

"Now, those ladies'll have to be told about its history too." Reminded Ardro. "Then they may want to come down to look at it. Can you give me a price quote? That might swing the deal if it's good enough."

They walked back into the air-conditioned office. The sudden chill, combined with the thrill of "Mission Accomplished," made Ardro shiver. He could hardly contain his private jubilation, as he salesman scribbled a set of figures on a piece of paper, and said, "Sir, this price is guaranteed to get 'em." And then he emphasized, "If you're sure they want to pay cash, my manager might be able to give them a even better deal than I can. One thing for sure he, and the police, will be glad to see some decent people take that van outa here."

The whole episode took less than twenty-five minute, and Ardro left the car lot with the hopeful salesman's price quote.

The black clothes, the heat and the sweat didn't bother him at all. He missed the bus, but that too didn't bother him. Ecstatic, he walked—almost ran—the two and a half miles back home. His relief—mixed with his pride, made his steps feel so light that he could have sailed over the moon. He had accomplished something he never thought that he'd be able to do.

Uncle Berty's admonitions from his childhood, "Don't let nothin' git ya'down." flashed through his mind. "Thanks, Uncle Berty," he thought as he felt pride in the fact that he had helped Mr. Dawson—he hoped successfully—and made Helene and Liddy proud of him.

For him this was a walk of victory.

That was an evening of rejoicing. Helene was sitting on the porch. When she saw him coming up the street, she could hardly believe that this was her son, Ardro, looking so handsome, mature and, confidant. "Thank God, He's O.K" she sighed.

He saw her sitting on the porch. He smiled, because he knew that ordinarily she wouldn't be out there at that time of day—it was too hot. She was waiting for him, and that made him feel good. He wanted to run, but he restrained himself, and he strode, almost nonchalantly towards the house. "Hi, Momma," He grinned

"My Goodness, don't you look pretty!" she acclaimed.

And, "Oh Ardro, you're so hot." She said with concern. "Did you walk all the way home? Why didn't ya ride the bus?"

Ardro soothed her. "Momma, I'm O.K. In fact I'm just fine. Although he was winded, and sweating from excitement and exhaustion, he said with all the spirit he could muster, "Yeah, Momma, I feel good. I did what I needed to do for Mr. Dawson."

"And Ya know, Momma, Uncle Berty woulda been proud of me. Even though I was scared to death, I put on a show. And it worked, Momma." He exalted.

Then he said with a hardy chuckle. "Momma, thanks for ya necklace and ring . . . Do I look like a little ol' lady?" Her laugh of delight, relief and joy could be heard even next door. "Lord No!" she shrieked. "You're beautiful. You're my beautiful young man, Ardro."

Their chat continued like this for a few more minutes. By this time, she had composed herself, and then she advised. "Now Ardro, you ought'a freshen up, Son. You're sweaty. I know you want to go see Liddy and Mrs. Dawson this evening. Beaming, she cooed, "I can't wait to see how she's going to act. After we eat something, we'll go over there."

Mrs. Dawson had been anxiously waiting for them to arrive. She and Liddy greeted them with delight. Ardro could see that she was happy and relaxed, but he could also see that she could hardly hold back her curiosity. He smiled, shaking his head as he watched her and Helene walk toward the den. "They'll be pickin' each other for information about what happened," he thought with amusement, as he and Liddy strolled off toward the back porch.

This was his first time on their back porch, and sitting close together on the back steps, he thought, "This would be a good time and place to kiss her." . . . What new and exciting end for his day!

Just as he was moving closer, she spoke. "Ardro," And she sidled up even closer to him on the step. "Today's the first time I've walked home by myself in a long time. The whole way home I kept thinking about what you must be doing. I think about you a lot now. I'm glad Daddy asked you to help him. Looks like you did it, too—whatever you set out to do—and I know Daddy's going to be happy. I know I am." She finished happily.

"Well I'm happy too," his face full of sunbeams. "But you don't know what I had to do," he teased. And giggling, "I had to dress up."

"Well, anyhow, Ardro, I bet you looked handsome," she giggled back.

"Yeah," he reflected happily. "It was kinda scary, but I figured out that it's not too hard to put on a good show." With a grin and a sigh of relief . . . "At least it's done."

Concerned then, he asked, "When's he coming home from the hospital? I want to tell'im face to face what's happened. I know that that could make everything all right for him. I hope he'll be able to come home soon."

Ardro could hardly contain himself.

They hadn't heard their mothers enter the kitchen. And it surprised them to hear Mrs. Dawson say, "I'm not sure what they mean, but the doctors called this morning, saying it might be Sunday before they could think of letting him come home." She was explaining to Helene that the doctors hoped to have Mr. Dawson's most intense anxiety attacks under control by Sunday.

Overhearing this, Ardro exclaimed aloud, "Sunday! Boy I was sure hoping I could tell him today."

He jumped up, and went to speak through the back door. "Uh, Mrs. Dawson, I know it would help him to get better if he knew I was able to do what he wanted. I don't have school tomorrow, can't I go over to the hospital first thing in the morning?"

"Oh Ardro, that would be so nice!" She exclaimed. "It's a great idea."

Helene nodded, with agreeable emphasis, that Ardro's visit could certainly help Mr. Dawson get out of the hospital sooner.

Liddy glowed, "Oh Ardro, you're brilliant. Pulling him back to the steps, she cooed. "Let's just sit and talk for a while before you have to go. Tomorrow's Saturday, so we don't have to study. Let's just enjoy each other for a while."

He finally got his kiss. This was the perfect end for a perfect day. He was on cloud nine.

His Saturday morning chores went undone. Helene let him slide because she wanted him to go to the hospital to see Mr. Dawson. She now knew how important Ardro's mission was for him.

Mr. Dawson had never been able to share with anyone, He had had to keep it all to himself. So Ardro was not surprised to hear that an anxiety attack had occurred just about the time the action was happening. He was happy, though, that Mr. Dawson was recovering from it.

Mr. Dawson was still under sedation when Ardro got there, and he had to wait a while before he could go to the room. "Now," he thought as he strode toward Mr. Dawson's room after nearly an hour's wait, "Now I can help bring Mr. Dawson back to his right mind with this news, and this concrete proof of my success."

Mr. Dawson was still groggy when Ardro entered. He was sitting up in bed, but his bright stare seemed vacant for a moment, and Ardro wasn't sure that Mr. Dawson recognized him. Just then, however, he broke into a wide grin. "I'm glad to see you, Ardro! Then clearly, and convincingly, he said to the nurse, "May I speak to this young man alone?"

The nurse finished her duties and left quietly.

"Oh Ardro, I'm so glad you came. Tell me—tell me . . . ." He was near tears.

"O.K. Mr. Dawson. You can take it easy now. Everything's O.K. now." Ardro assured him as he stood close to the bed. "Let me tell you what happened."

"Yeah?"

"I got it!" Exclaimed Ardro.

Without a word Mr. Dawson fell back on the bed, and seemed momentarily to go into a deep sleep.

"Mr. Dawson, wake up. What happened?" Yelled Ardro. And he rushed over to check on him. When he touched him, he could feel his body shaking. Ardro then realized that, with relief, Mr. Dawson was weak with delight.

He sat down in the bedside chair, put his head on the bed, and tears of joy and gratitude came to his eyes too.

Soon, he felt Mr. Dawson's hand on his head. Neither spoke or moved for a full minute. Then, as he straightened up, he placed both envelopes on the bed and proudly said, "Mr. Dawson, here's what you've been looking for."

Mr. Dawson picked up the parchment-like envelope, looked at it, and started crying again, grinning and laughing—all at the same time.

"Oh Ardro, M'Boy, You're my lifesaver!"

Ardro was so overwhelmed with joy he could hardly speak. "I'm glad I could do it." He whispered.

They both sat silent. At that time, with a confused look on his face, Mr. Dawson picked up the other envelope.

"What's this?" he asked.

"I don't know. I found it underneath one of the other seats. That was the first one I found."

Mr. Dawson looked inside. Really puzzled, he gasped, and uttered in alarm, "I don't know what this stuff is Ardro, My God, it looks dangerous. It sure didn't come from NCB. This stuff looks really illegal."

"Oh Jeez, Mr. Dawson," yelped Ardro, "where'd it come from?"

"Humn." Buzzed Mr. Dawson in deep thought. He got agitated again. Then after a couple of frowning minutes he brightened up, and said tentatively, "Well Ardro, Ya' know? Now I'm beginning to remember. Things are beginning to come back to me.

He took another moment to compose himself.

"Ardro, Remember what I told about that night you first saw me? I watched those guys fooling around with that van. I told you about that, didn't I?"

"Yeah, Mr. Dawson you sure did."

"Well, it's really coming back to me now. Evidently Ardro, they must have got in it, and stashed my formula in it then. And they probably stashed this stuff in there too."

And then—like a lightening bolt—it hit him. "Ardro, this stuff may be some that 'acid' they were peddling!"

Ardro felt chilled. "Omigod! Ya really think so, Mr. Dawson?"

"Well, I don't know, but it could be."

"Whadaya gonna do with it?" Asked Ardro anxiously.

Mr. Dawson began to feel the tightness coming back. He flopped back on his bed. "Ooh!" he signed. "Yeah," he thought, "what AM I going to do with it?"

For the first time in a long time, he prayed. "Please God, Help me. I can't let Ardro get caught with this stuff, and there's no way I can tell NCB the whole story about the way I got it. Recovering that formula is supposed to be detective work that I assigned—successfully."

Ardro's head was whirling. At the same time, he was considering, "Man if I try to get rid of that stuff, I might get caught with it." There'd be nothing I could say, because my fingerprints are all over the bag. I can' t tell nobody where I got it, 'cause that would undo all the stuff I did to help Mr. Dawson."

Each of them, in their own thoughts, felt devastated, scared and sad. Ardro certainly didn't want to see Mr. Dawson have a relapse over this. Both sat in panicky silence again, with their thoughts racing to find an answer to the dilemma they faced.

"Mr. Dawson," said Ardro finally, "Maybe I shoulda just left it there."

Mr. Dawson shook he head, and passionately said, "Uhn uhn! No Ardro! No! Remember? That van was mine, and I wouldn't want it found there."

"Oooh yeah!" Responded Ardro,—Well, We have to find a way,"

After a long pause Mr. Dawson sat up again. This time, he seemed calm and collected. He finally said very deliberately, "I think I've got it, Ardro. I think we both—you and I—ought to get the credit for recovering that formula."

"Uh, You mean me, too?" Brightened Ardro.

"Yep, you too, Ardro. If it hadn't been for you, I'd still be in hot water—Huh! I guess I still am, until I can get out of here and let them know the good news." Chuckled, Mr. Dawson. "But that other stuff—it could get us into big trouble if we don't handle this right."

"O.K. What do WE do?" He asked. Feeling excited.

Mr. Dawson, his mind now keen and functioning again, said, "Well, we can't get rid of it. It's off the street now, and we can't let it go back out there, so I've decided . . . ."

"I'll turn in this envelope, along with the illegal drugs, as if I confiscated them at the same time I recovered the envelope. I won't even have to burn the envelope, because your fingerprints are on it legitimately. We'll both get credit for retrieving it."

"Hey, that's cool, Mr. Dawson. Looks like you're back in it again." said Ardro, excited as he sat back in the chair and—for the first time—took a good long look at Mr. Dawson.

Mr. Dawson was staring back at him, and they both liked what they saw.

* * *

VIII

Recharged

Ardro left the hospital, once again feeling like he was floating just above the sidewalk. Although he couldn't yet tell everything to Helene, he had something he could share—something that was good. As he strode along, carefully rehearsing exactly what he wanted to say, and how he would tell it, his thoughts were interrupted by—

"Hey Ardro!"—A voice he hadn't heard for a while.

He pivoted as he recognized an almost forgotten sound catching up with him.

"Squeaky! You ol' spook." He yelped. "Whatcha' been doin'? "Boy! I didn't expect it to be you, but I could hear ya comin.'"

"Well, You haven't been lookin' for any of my hook-ups, Ardro." Chided Squeaky, as they strolled along. "Ya just been outa my loop.

"Yeah, I been dodgin' em." He joked back.

"Well, O.K. I'm stayin' busy anyway . . . . Hey, did ya get back in school?"

"Sure did Squeaky. I got back, and I'm doin' pretty well, too. I had a turn-around since I last saw you, Squeaky. Made up my mind to do it right this time."

"Right-on, Ardro. I'm glad for ya.

The next thing Squeaky said surprised Ardro. "Ardro, I Wish I could make up my mind before it's too late. Really Man, this stuff I'm doin' out here aint right. I oughta get back in there too, and hang with it. Too many of us guys are fallin' off the tracks . . . . And Man, I can stay on the tracks, I don't have to fall off."

"Yeah," He continued as he reflected with resolve, "I've really been thinking about it. It's tough out here."

At this point, Squeaky couldn't stop talking. "Hummn, I guess you heard about ol' Shack, didn't ya? Heard he did-in some guy with 'acid', and got laid up in jail."

"Yep." Answered Ardro matter-of-factly, "I thought you had heard, Squeaky. The guy that got did-in was me . . . . Almost finished me off too."

"Omigod! You?" gasped Squeaky.

"Yeah me, Man. And that's what turned me around. I was a lucky dude, Squeaky." Said Ardro. "I was lucky. I pulled through, and I'm doing O.K. now. It's a long story".

"Man! I wanna hear your story, Ardro and I wanna talk to ya,. When can we get together?" He was almost pleading.

"Well, pretty soon, Squeaky I hope—as long as you don't try to sell me any of your girls," Ardro teased.

"Aaahh! O.K. Ardro," giggled Squeaky. "Yeah, and I heard you got your own girl friend now, so I won't worry you with that." He smiled as Ardro turned to go.

"That's a part of what's happening. In fact, a lotta stuff's happenin' right now, and I wanna tell ya all about it when I get a chance. Things look pretty good, too but right now I gotta get home." He began to walk away, but he turned and said, "Squeaky, it was good to see ya. Keep thinkin' about school. We'll keep in touch.

"O.K. Well good luck, Ardro. Good Luck Pal." Squeaky handed him a piece of paper. "Here's my phone number. Give me a call as soon as you can. Maybe we can help each other. O.K?"

This chance meeting with Squeaky played in Ardro's head the rest of the way home. It made him think about his own future. "Right now, it looks pretty upbeat." He thought, as he bounded through the door expecting Helene to be standing at the window.

Instead, he saw her napping in a living-room chair.

"Hey, Momma," he sang as he bounded through the door. "I got a lotta stuff I can tell ya now. C'mon, wake up!"

Helene wasn't napping. When she heard him come up on the porch, she quickly sat back and tried to fake it, just to keep from grabbing and hugging him. She didn't want him to think that she was overanxious; She just wanted to hear the good news. Ardro's greeting thrilled her so, that even with her eyes closed, she knew that she couldn't hide a smile, or stay still. Brightly, she sat up so suddenly that he flinched.

She cackled with a hearty laugh, "Oh Honey! I'm so glad you're home. Sit down, cool off and tell me all about it."

Ardro hesitated.

Then overexcited, she pleaded, "Out with it Ardro. I can hardly wait. How'd it go?"

He stood still for a long minute—until it looked like that she was going to burst. Then with a big grin he blurted,

"Momma, Do you think, I'd make a good detective?"

"Huh?"

Her shock made him laugh heartily.

"Yeah, ha ha, Momma! I caught ya off guard, didn't I?

"Well, yeah, ya sure did." She giggled. Then with a serious look on her face, she asked, "What'cha talkin' 'bout, boy?"

He didn't go into the whole story, but he began my telling about the big van.

"Momma, you know, this big yella gold van everybody's been talkin' about?"

"Yeah, what about it?

"Well, ya' know—according to the grapevine—its been involved in a lotta the strange happenings on the street. It could'a even been the cause of Cartel dyin'. And Momma, I found out a lot about it."

"Humn, Go on, Boy."

"And Momma, did ya know that Mr. Dawson works for the Pharmaceutical Company?"

"No—, Uh, well yeah, I'd heard he worked in drugs. But them's clean drugs, right?

"Yeah, Momma. That's the big medicine factory 'cross town."

"O.K. Now I'm beginning to see how people are saying he might be mixed up in this mess."

He's involved, all right, Momma, but in the right way. And that's what I've been helping with.

Then, without going into much detail, he finally told how he had helped Mr. Dawson solve his problem. He recounted his part in helping recover the drugs and the papers.

So proud that he could have screamed, Helene sat with her mouth hanging open in stone silence.

He finished his story. Then, with conviction, he said, "Ya' know Momma, after the last few days, I been doing a lotta stuff that got me to doing some real deep thinking. I'm pretty sure I could make a real good detective; and, you know what? I'm a medicine man too."

"A Medicine man! Now, how do ya' mean 'you're a medicine man', too?" She quizzed.

With great emotion, he said, "I just might save a whole lot of people's lives."

With a smile that brightened the whole room, he told her. "Momma, with your gold chain, ya cross and some pretty smooth moves, I got what I was supposed to. And I didn't break any laws either." Jubilantly he finished—"and what I did, made Mr. Dawson feel a whole lot better. He's better now, ain't he? He'll probably come home tomorrow. I'm a Medicine man!"

"And—And" He continued. "Ya know Momma, I was just about like a detective." . . . Then, after a pensive pause, he said enthusiastically, "And ya know what Momma? Bein' a detective is just what I wanna do when I finish school. "And—And,"—He was excited. "Wouldn't that be great?

"With all them 'Ands' you serious, ain't you, Boy?" Said an impressed Helene.

"Yep, I am, AND, when I'm finished school, I'm goin' to college. And soon too!"

Helene fought back tears of happiness. "Oh, I'm so proud of you, Ardro." She hugged him tightly, sat back and just beamed. This was enough for her. She didn't need to ask any more questions. She realized that Ardro's accomplishment had been better than she could ever have dreamed. He'd done such a good thing, and she was happy.

"God!" She breathed, in a long relaxed prayerful sigh, "Thank you, Lord. And please help him get what he wants outa life."

Ardro's happiness at that moment surpassed any he had ever experienced. For him it was a rare moment of self-realization and possibilities. He felt overwhelmed with pride and determination. He closed his eyes and shouted aloud—to contemplative Helene—"Monday morning!"

Tears filled her eyes. She just listened.

"Monday morning," He repeated, "I gotta really start getting ready for school. Before school starts in the fall, I gotta get a job, and work hard again—even during the year. I gotta catch up. I don't wanna get off the track again."

Helene sat quiet, with an unopened magazine in her lap, just looking at him, feeling her love and pride spill over into her real nature of "wantin' to do somthin'."

"And Ardro," she finally and resolutely said, "I'm gonna do whatever it takes to help you make it happen."

The more he thought of being a law officer; the more the idea appealed to him.

"Momma," He interrupted their separate enchantment. "You know, I'm really serious about the idea of doin' police work. Not just a regular street cop, but a secret undercover man, where I can really pull off somethin'—like finding out what's ruining our neighborhood—what's makin' our boys bad.

The rest of the evening was a delight for both of them. For the first time in a long time, they were comfortable, relaxed and at peace. Twists, turns and bumps at the horizon of the road to success did not concern them now. They blithely discussed his finishing school, going to a police academy and training for undercover work; helping to keep drugs off the streets and making life easier for the kids in the neighborhood. Although he figured that it would take a long time to realize this newfound dream, he then went to bed, very happy and excited about it

It was a beautiful Saturday evening.

The next morning—Sunday morning—came too soon for Ardro. He had slept like a log, but woke up with the uneasy feeling that going to church wouldn't be a very good thing to do this particular morning. He said so when he got up, and again at the breakfast table. So Helene didn't urge him. She left without him.

His uneasiness was justified. Helene was almost sorry that she was there. He would have been miserable.

What she observed as she entered the church confirmed Ardro's dread. Mrs. Morris, Cartel's mother was there, and was surrounded by a covey of comforting white-frocked ladies. She sighed and wept as Pastor Kirkwood's long sermon—with many Bible verses and platitudes—tried to pacify her mourning. Many songs were sung, and many prayers were said. But during the entire long service, hardly anything was said about the conditions in that community that allowed Cartel's death to happen. There was no mention, that for years the neighborhood covered up and provided safe haven for criminal activities, and still allowed dreadful things, like what happened to Cartel, to go on—over and over again—to kids. Nothing was said about what the church might do to guide kids away from such fates, and towards good futures.—Only praying, singing and a lot of weeping!

It was only after church was out—and in the crowd-mix out in front—that people talked about the awful conditions that brought about the drug bust, the consequent chase, and Cartel's death when he ran out into the street after getting hold of that stuff.

Helene, with her friend Tina, solemnly walked away from the crowd.

"Oh," She moaned. "I feel so sorry for Cartel's mother."

With disgust for what they had just experienced, she said, "Ya see Tina, maybe if Cartel, and his buddies, had had a chance to come to this church and work with people who could help them, he wouldn'ta been taken away from his mother so soon. Oh, I Wish this church would do somethin' for our kids!"

"Yeah." answered heartbroken Tina, . . . "Maybe my Bernetta coulda' been saved too, and found her way."

"Well anyway," said Helene, with renewed and defiant determination, "from now on we can't be wishy-washy no longer, Tina. At least, **I**'ve got to make something happen for my boy—something good." She emphasized.

Meanwhile, Ardro didn't get out of bed until just before noon. He spent the morning, lying there wondering what was being said about Cartel at church. He just about knew.

At any rate, his sadness and concern about Cartel didn't cut into his other thoughts—his excitement about his decision to finish school and be a detective. His mind was still keyed up, because he was still processing his plans for his future.

He wasn't in a hurry to leave the house, but he was restless. So, even without any breakfast, he decided to take a walk down the street while Helene was at church.

He had leisurely strolled for about two blocks, when suddenly; the high-pitch roar of a car, approaching at high speed from the rear, interrupted his thoughts. There were really two cars. One was chasing the other. As he watched, he recognized the second car as one belonging to Cody Mongus, Mr. Mongus' oldest son.

"Wow", He thought. "What in the world could be happenin' now? This is Sunday morning." And then, just as the two cars rounded the corner of 14th St. two blocks away, a third car, a police car, joined the chase from another direction.

He was curious, but he didn't hurry. But by the time he got to 14th St. there was nothing special to see—but there was plenty to hear. A group of his school buddies were huddled there in deep discussion about what they had heard, and some of them had seen. He casually joined the huddle, and listened to their shocking chitchat.

According to them, "Cody Mongus, caught some guy on the street, and almost killed him" They didn't know what it was all about. "The cops hauled 'em both away."

"Big shot Kid's in trouble now!" they crowed. One of them said, "Think he got cut too, 'cause he was bleedin'."

Ardro didn't say anything. He just listened. Then after he picked up what he could out of the conversation, he strolled away thinking, "Wow! This is really strange. Hummn, even Cody's got problems. Glad I'm not in his shoes. I wonder what he did?"

Maybe Momma's heard something at church. Boy! If she did, she'll be bustin' with either gossip or questions. I'll see when she gets home."

"Wonder how Mr. Mongus is going to take this."

Helene hadn't heard a thing about what Ardro had seen and heard during his walk. Instead, as she meandered home from church, her head was reeling with ideas and thoughts about her and Ardro's needs, and his friend's, "Where are they gonna get the support and backing they need to finish school and be successful?" She asked herself aloud. "Who can help?" Then, for the hundredth time, she came to the awesome realization that, she, herself, is going to be helpless without somebody who has some clout in the neighborhood, and in the city. "But, Who?" she asked herself. "Who can I see first? Help's got to come from somebody—

"Hummmm, Mr. Mongus?" She thought. Almost immediately, she remembered her past encounters with him. "Nah" she smiled to herself. "I might kill'im."

She had become so wrapped up in her own thoughts and plans that she overlooked the fact that Ardro was thinking about the same thing. She had forgotten that he might want to find his own way, and make his own plans.

In this frame of mind, she hurried into the house to find that Ardro had already left. Disappointed, she grumbled, "Where'd that boy go now?" "It's too early for him to go over to Liddy's. Tsk! Oh well, I'll just fix some lunch. Sure hope he comes home quick, 'cause I wanna talk to 'im."

Before long, she heaved a sigh of satisfaction when she heard him come in. "Momma! You here?"

"Ha! Yeah Baby, I'm here in the kitchen. C'mon back I wanna talk to ya."

He strolled in gingerly, and flopped down at the table. "Hi Momma. How was church?'

"Oh church was nice." She said. But hesitantly, "Miss Tina and I both were feeling awful when we left." Then she added sadly, "Poor Cartel's mom had a real hard time.

With disgust, she continued. "And ya' know? Nobody got any hope outa that service. Things ain't gonna git no better for kids in this neighborhood."

Understanding, Ardro nodded his head, then suddenly asked "Was Mr. Mongus there?"

"Mr. Mongus!" exclaimed Helene. "Mr. Mongus don't go to our church. He goes to some church with the high muckety-mucks."

"Yeah, well Humn—." He thought out loud. "I wonder if he went to his church this morning."

Helene's antennae went up. "Why are you askin' about Mr. Mongus, Ardro?" She probed.

"Well, I just heard something. Just now—out on the street."

She rushed toward him. "What? What'ja hear?"

"O.K. Momma," He chuckled. Turn off the stove and sit down. We don't wanna burn up the food."

Without another word she hastily sat down on the edge of a chair, and listened intently—her mouth open—gulping down everything he said. It tickled him to see her so bowled over by gossip. He told her the story about all he had seen and heard while he was walking—the chase, the police and about Cody.—.

"Cody? Ya mean Mr. Mongus' Cody?" she interrupted. "What about 'im?"

"He was in the car doing the chasing." Finished Ardro. "Right now that's all I know, Momma. I thought you might 'a heard something from somebody on the way home. I was hoping you'd be able to tell me something"

"Oh My God! She exclaimed. "No Ardro, this is the first I've heard. And, weirdly, I was just thinking about Mr. Mongus on the way home."

"Well, you're gonna hear lots more, Momma."

"Oh lord! This is brand new to me, she declared. A whole new angle for me. I can't stop thinking about what Mr. Mongus must be going through right now."

"Now THAT is strange!" She mulled jovially to herself. "Up to now he's aggravated the hell outa me, and right now, I'm feelin' a tinge 'a pity—wondering how he's takin' a little bit 'a tough luck."

All afternoon, thoughts about the Mongus family kept bugging her. "Wow, I wonder how he's gonna face the public tomorrow. After all his braggin' 'bout his kids I'm sure he'll be shamefaced. Humn, I kinda feel sorry for him."

It surprised her that she felt genuinely concerned about him. With her mind temporarily off of him as a source of help, she wondered. "What kinda trouble is Cody in?"

Ardro's thoughts meanwhile, were never far from his newly found vision of detective. His curiosity really got the best of him. And in relation to this incident, he couldn't stop thinking,

"Gosh, Wow! What if?" New thoughts were flashing through his head." Humn,—I oughta try looking into this thing and find out what really happened. There's somethin' really screwy's going on."

Helene was still talking, but he wasn't listening. Instead his thoughts kept coming. "Man! I'm sure surprised to see Cody get into that kinda mess. I'd sure like to find out why." His musings surprised him. And he had the sudden thought, "Maybe I can. I don't want to be nosy, but maybe there'd be something I could do to help him. I don't know'im, all that well, but I really would like to help—especially since I know his brother Hugh, from school."

—"School!" This called his mind back.

"School," He repeated out loud. "By Golly, I almost forgot!" "Huh, I gotta keep myself on track. I can't sidetrack from school now, 'cause if I'm going to be that detective, I've got to get back in there and finish up."

At that point his thoughts began to match Helene's.

Alert again, he said. "Momma, I'm just thinkin', Cody might be in deep trouble." With a slight nod of her head, she looked at him in agreement. "Humn!" he went on, "Ya know Momma, . . . Maybe this all fits together in some strange way. You been tryin' get Mr. Mongus to give me a job so I can get back in school, and now,—." He smiled a little eloquent smile.

"Maybe if I could help Cody just like I helped Mr. Dawson, Mr. Mongus might soften up a little bit. Yeah! And now maybe Momma, . . . just maybe, what I've found out by working with Mr. Dawson could help Cody and his Daddy. And maybe Mr. Mongus could even help me get back into school."

"Oh Ardro, Git outta here!" Helene retorted with gleeful surprise at Ardro's proposal. "But, ya know, ya might be right." She grinned. As these ideas were running through their heads, he realized then, that he was going to need some serious help to do it.

Almost immediately, the Dawsons were the first one's he thought about. He sensibly considered "They're the most logical contact. And my chances are real good that Mr. Dawson would help me find out what I want to know. He'd be sure to have some ideas, and he'd really know how to get information from the police". "Yep, but just like before, even with Mr. Dawson's direction, I'd have to be tricky, and smart; just like when I searched that van.

"Yeah, He knows Liddy likes me, and I know he'll help. I'm gonna go see him." He said to himself as he walked along, grinning happily. "But I'll wait until tomorrow morning to contact Him—for the 'real' help I need."

Sunday evening went quickly. Though he slept lightly, he was up at the crack of dawn on Monday morning. He rushed over to the Dawsons just at the time he thought they might be getting out of bed. Liddy answered the door. "Ardro! You're sure up early."

"Yeah. Hi Liddy! He said cheerily. I've been thinkin' about you all night.

"Well, why are you over here now?"

With a sly smile, "Well, it seems such a long time between times I see you; what's it been?—Two—three nights ago?"

She giggled. "I missed you too, Ardro. But I'm going to school. Why come here so early?"

"I just stopped by to check on things, and tell you what a good time I had last night. And something else; I might not be able to walk you home today.

What's up, Ardro? What's going on?

Well, Liddy, ya' see, I had a hard time sleeping last night, but while I was layin' there, I did decide to make a move. I just couldn't wait to tell ya'.—Liddy, after school,

I'm going to the office to talk to Mr. Brevard about what I need to get in order get in college." He declared. "Momma's coming along too . . . I'm serious now, Liddy. We're makin' plans."

"Oh Ardro, my heart's so happy for you. You've made the decision I wanted you to make, and I know you'll be happy.—" We'll be happy! Oh, I'm so thrilled. Don't worry, I can find my way home. "She smiled."

"I wanna be happy for a long time with you, Liddy." Ardro beamed. He felt so proud.

"We'll graduate together. Won't that be great?"

He nodded, and smiled self-assuredly. "But right now Liddy, I've got to do something." He added. "I also wanted to see how Mr. Dawson's doin', and when he's coming home. I've got to ask him a couple 'a questions if he feels like talking."

"Well Ardro, he's doing a lot better now." Liddy said brightly, "The doctors tell us that he should be home in a couple of days."

"O.K. Great!" He backed away saying. "Gotta hurry now. I know Momma's wondering where I went this early. Talk to you at school, if I can get a chance."

Helene had guessed where he went, and had a light breakfast for him. "Don't you be late, Boy" She admonished when he left for school

That Monday was a busy day for them both. Helene's curiosity was killing her, so she spent most of the morning trying to find out more neighborhood gossip. She spent almost an hour on the phone with anybody she could think of that would give a bit of news. All she heard was that Cody was back home before mid-afternoon, the Mongus' house was like a fortress and, that the police were all around; allowing no one else to come near.

Meanwhile, Ardro stopped for fleeting chats with Liddy—when he met her in the hall, in between classes.

On of those times he had a chance to ask, "Liddy, have you heard anything about what's been happening over at the Mongus'?"

"Yeah," Liddy answered musingly. "Surprising, isn't it?"

"Well, . . . I got this feeling, Liddy—It's funny . . ." I never knew Cody that well . . . and Mr. Mongus sure has been a pain in the neck for Momma—But I wanna help if I can," He shared. "'Cause Hugh's a buddy of mine, and I haven't seen much of him this summer." With a snicker, "I guess they ain't let 'im out."

On another one of their chats, He spoke earnestly. "I wanna talk with ya', Liddy, after Momma and I finish up at school today, Can I come over?"

"Well," She answered. "You know my Mom's at his office now. I'll have to check with her. I think it'll be O.K. though, because I'll tell her you want to help Cody and Hugh. And, she'll like that."

Helene spent most of the rest of the afternoon on the phone with Tina. After she had gathered all she could from the other neighbors, she finally called Tina, and Tina gave her an earful.

She listened in awe as Tina revealed: "Helene, at one time, Cody was friendly with Bernetta, he'd always treated her kindly—almost like a sister—and protected her from thugs in the street. I guess that's why I'm so upset now that he's in trouble."

Tina continued. "You know, Helene, I don't like Mr. Mongus any more than you do, but I sure would like to find out how I can help Cody."

Helene was surprised to hear this, and she continued to listen. She found out more interesting stuff from Tina, but reluctantly, she had to leave the long, interesting conversation to meet Ardro at school for the conference he'd scheduled.

Ardro had contentedly finished his classes for that day. He and Liddy were standing at the end of the walkway when she arrived.

"See ya' later Liddy." He waved.

Helene was all a-chatter, as they walked toward the office. She relayed to Ardro some of the gossip she picked up from Tina, and what was circulating the community. He listened, but not closely, as they strolled toward Mr. Browne's office.

All of a sudden, his ears perked when she began to tell him the tale:

"Miss Tina gave me the dirty details, Ardro, She told me that a street dude named Ronnie had snatched a wallet from Cody, and that Cody chased him down to get the wallet back."

"A wallet—just a wallet?" Ardro puzzled. "Wonder what scared Cody so bad that he'd chase down Ronnie Cook, in a car-chase on a quiet Sunday afternoon for—just a wallet?"

"Well, according to Tina, it seems like the wallet had more than money in it. It appears that Ronnie wanted to get something on Cody. The kids in the street all been sayin' that Ronnie's really got—it—in for Mr. Mongus."

"Ya," said Ardro. I heard that too, but I don't know why.

"Well Ardro, Tina told me. Ronnie just got outa jail, and he blames Mr. Mongus for puttin' him there. "Huh!" She huffed. "I'm not surprised at that. Mr. Mongus was so ugly to a lotta people."

She continued, "They say, this Dude was renting a "pad"—a nice one too—from Mr. Mongus. But then when Mr. Mongus found out that a lotta Gays, prostitutes and druggies hung out there, he had that house raided. Everybody in it went to jail one night."

"Au Oh!" Thought Ardro, as he listened intently to Helene's informative prattle "Things are warming up.—Dag-blast-it!" His mind wrestled. "Wish I was a detective now! I could really find out what's goin' on for Cody. Humn . . . well, I guess that's the reason I'm on my way to the principal right now—to learn how to do it."

With this in mind, he had missed some of what Helene was saying.

"What's that again, Momma? I got sidetracked on thinkin' about school and detective work—Someway I could help Cody."

She retold the tale about how Ronnie went to jail. By the time she had finished, they were nearing the office.

Brody Browne saw them approaching. He watched their animated conversation with satisfaction, and then he called Mr. Brevard the counselor, and Mrs. Coursin down to his office so that the three of them could support each other. During their greetings, he praised the marked change in Helene. Both he and Mr. Brevard seemed delighted to see such a change in both of them.

Mr. Brevard reported that Ardro had done very well during Summer school, and, best of all, that his prolonged absence from school for suspension would not affect his standing.

"We expect him back in the fall, and he should definitely be able to graduate with his class, if he keeps up."

Ardro felt overjoyed, and enthusiastically shared his vision and what he had decided to do for a career. "Mr. Browne," He asserted. "A lotta my buddies have quit, and, right now, they're gettin' into trouble on the street. And since I've been out there with them, I think I know why. "There's too much out there that they can't handle; all kind of drugs & stuff. And the cops don't know how to get to the problem."

At this point he began to share his dream.

"Well Mr. Browne, I wanna be a cop—a secret cop—so I can find out how to stop the waste and killin."

Now that he had started talking, he just couldn't stop. "I know I'm compelled to go on and finish school now—" He continued,—"'cause I want to go on to college and learn how to do 'real' police work. The kind that finds out what the problems are—and helps put stops on them." He talked on for more than a minute, saying things that he had been thinking about, but never expressed out loud to anybody.

With radiant smiles, they all sat and listened to Ardro, very affected by what they were hearing. Helene's hands were clasped in thankful praise.

Mr. Brevard finally spoke—with emotion that surprised him.—"Ardro, your turn-around has been so impressive, that I know that Mr. Browne, all the counselors, all your teachers, and I, will do all we can to give you the help you need next year—and even afterward, to meet your goals, if need be."

Mr. Browne, put his hand on Ardro's shoulder, "Ardro, all you need to do, is do your best." And then he shook his hand, genially saying, "We're with you all the way, Ardro. God Bless you."

Ardro felt like a true Knight!

Helene's looks of adoration impressed Brody so, that he was gratified to comment again, about the change in her outlook on her life, and on Ardro.

The after-school conference made both of them happy. The meeting was a total success.

As he watched them leaving the building, Brody had a fantasy that he saw them gleefully skipping arm in arm down the sidewalk.

After the conference, they walked home together, and as they discussed their happy review of the conference, Ardro suddenly interjected, "Momma, I been thinking. Ya' know, Mr. Dawson helped point me to the way I wanna go in life, now maybe he'll give me some detective pointers about how to find out what really happened to Cody. I know he'd knows how, and I'm pretty sure he'd help me."

"And that it'd make it easier to get some help from Mr. Mongus""

The first remark took some of the shine off Helene's mood. "Oh Ardro, maybe you ought to back off 'a that. Ya' got so much to do in school." But when she heard his last comment, about Mr. Mongus being grateful, she reconsidered, "Yeah, ya might be right boy."

Little more was said about it before they got home. The rest of the walk was a delight.

As soon as they got home, he left again, promising that he'd be home for dinner—headed straight for the Dawsons house. At the Dawsons, peacefully and quietly, he continued his conversations with Liddy where he happily shared the events of his meeting at school.

And, of course, this happy conversation led to the real reason he wanted to visit. He wanted, so much to finish his talk with her Daddy.

"This has to get done right away." He said. "—And then too maybe Mrs. Dawson could help, since she knows them so well." He added.

Liddy quickly let him know that Mrs. Dawson didn't want to interfere.

"Mother really doesn't think she should talk about the Mongus Family information. I think she's scared of them," giggled Liddy.

"Yeah, I can see that." He grinned. Well anyway, be sure to let Mr. Dawson know that I wanna to talk with him.

A lot of homework was calling, and he knew Helene was fixing dinner. So as he hugged Liddy, he said, "Well Liddy, I wish I could stay longer, but I gotta go." After a short chat, he left for home. With a cheerily sly smile and a wave, she assured him. "Daddy will be glad to help too, I know!"

Ardro was determined. Now, more than ever, he was unwavering in his decision.

He's got Liddy, a nice girl friend. He's got a clear-cut direction to go. He's got guts from Uncle Berty. He's got good friends in the Dawsons, and best of all, He's got a Momma that "Ain't helpless No More!!!" She's going to do everything she can to help him.

* * *

IX

On The Way

It was Friday. He was ecstatic that Mr. Dawson was home from the hospital. As soon they heard, he and Helene went over for a visit. It was a joyous occasion. The Dawsons were happy to see him. For the first time, they both hugged him, as they congratulated him for making his "grown-up" decisions. They had become confident that Ardro would become a success, and they let him know that they would help him in whatever way they could.

He'd never seen him Mr. Dawson so well and happy before, and it made him happy. He adoringly watched Liddy's glowing pleasure. And, for the first time in his life, he felt truly satisfied with himself. Helene sat, observing the whole scene with tears of bliss dampening her blouse.

He and Mr. Dawson made it to the back porch later that evening, and there he shared his thoughts. It was heartwarming talking—man to man—with Mr. Dawson; Ardro'd never been able to do that before, either. His Daddy was never really around, and Uncle Berty—even though he gave good advice—was "kinda wacky." This experience was a brand new one for him, and it made him feel enormously pleased.

Finally, he got around to his mission—his chance to explain to Mr. Dawson the situation about the Mongus family. He passed along, the story as told to him on the way to the school on Monday morning by Helene. Mr. Dawson had heard about Cody, but he too, didn't know much about what had happened. He had been asking questions.

Then he called Mrs. Dawson out, to see if she would shed any light on the story.

She prudently showed her reluctance to talk, by stating, "They keep their distance, you know. They've always been so high-minded about their kids. According to them, all three of them 'can do no wrong'. And this thing must truly be driving them crazy."

"Especially now," She continued, as she revealed. "Cody, the oldest is getting ready to get married. For months this family's been planning the biggest wedding this community has seen in years".

"Oh Boy, this really is gonna be a mess." Thought Ardro.

"Well, we're all here together now." Said Mr. Dawson. "Let's all talk about it."

He called Helene. She and Liddy joined them. He asked her to retell what she had told Ardro. With her story, and with what Liddy had heard from her friends, they began to piece together the details of what had happened to Cody and the Mongus family.

That afternoon, right there on the Dawsons back porch; they agreed that it would be the right thing for them all to try to do something for the Mongus family. Helene reluctantly and huffily accepted the fact that it was a good idea. "Especially, since it might help Ardro get some money." She thought.

The next morning, Mr. Dawson woke up thinking about what Ardro wanted to do. He was feeling quite well,

"Liddy," he asked. Would you please call Ardro for me? Ask him to come over as soon as he can.

"Oh, O.K. Daddy. Will he—?" She started expectantly.

"No," He chuckled. "He won't have time to go to the park with you. Both of you have homework, and, He and I've got things to do"

She called. Ardro came, on the fly, because that Friday afternoon, and the night before, he had talked with some of his street buddies at school, and heard a lot about a few more very interesting facts. Using what they had, and from what he had learned, he now felt ready to convince Mr. Dawson to help him with some good detective skills. "Because that's what I wanna do, and I'm gonna be good at it." He vowed silently.

And he was sincere, and determined. to be successful in helping Cody out. Not just because Mr. Mongus might be able to do something for him, but also because he liked Hugh, and because he'd feel bad, if all his efforts went sour.

Mr. Dawson was glad that Ardro wanted to investigate, but he had reservations about Ardro's lack of skill. "He might cause more trouble than help." He thought. However, Ardro kept saying, "I can talk to the guys in the street, and I can find out stuff you can't, Mr. Dawson."

So, the first thing Mr. Dawson said was "Ardro I think you're right. I think if we really want to help Cody, the first thing we have to do is to get the story straight—Get the facts. And, looking Ardro squarely in the eye, "Ardro, the only way to do that is to go directly to him, and ask him. You can help by doing that, Ardro.

"O Good Lord, Mr. Dawson," He gasped. "I can't to that." Now, he realized the contradiction of what he had just said. "He probably won't even talk to me. I don't know him that well. He knows I'm in his little brother's class, but he don't really know who I am."

"But I'll be along with you, Ardro, said Mr. Dawson. Let's you and I go together to ask him. He knows what I do, and if I offer to give him some help to get out of this pickle, I'm sure I can get him to meet us someplace for a talk. You'll know a whole lot more about what he's talking about than I will, so both of us together may be able to make some sense out this for him.

"Hummn! You help me, and I help him. Is that it?" His confidence returning.

"That's it," Affirmed Mr. Dawson.

They met with Cody at 10:30 on Saturday morning at an old building, in an out-of-the-way room Mr. Dawson used as his "office" for his undercover work,

Cody was very nervous and wary, but Mr. Dawson soon put him at ease. It was only after he was assured that theirs was a sincere effort to salvage his reputation, and to ease his family trauma, that he began to relax. Only then did he begin the conversation about what was troubling him.

Neither of them anticipated the story that followed.

They both realized that strange and awesome things happen to young people in the neighborhood. They were surprised, however, that Cody Mongus, had been dawn into such a bizarre set of circumstances

For a full minute, Cody sat silent. Mr. Dawson and Ardro waited patiently. Then, without warning he put his head down on the table, and started to cry. Shocked and embarrassed at this spectacle, they sympathetically listened as Cody lifted his head, and tearfully began his strange story of how he got involved in something that he was totally unprepared for.

He revealed to them that several weeks ago, during a night out on the town he, and a couple of his buddies were joined by a guy he knew only as Ronnie Cook, a mere acquaintance. He never really liked Ronnie, because he could never understand why Ronnie hated his Daddy, Mr. Mongus. It was of no real concern to him, but he casually joined in a conversation, hoping to perhaps find out why.

"The other two left." He said. "But I sat there, just chattin', and Ronnie offered to buy me a drink. I was surprised." He said.—"I didn't expect that. I knew he didn't like my Daddy, but I hadn't done anything to him. So I accepted it, and we kept on talking."

I didn't realize at the time, what I was in for."—"Pretty soon though," He moaned, "and before I knew it, I went into a "high" like I'd never felt before."

"And I got stone cold."

He continued with a shiver. "I could just barely hear the music. The room got bigger. The lights got dimmer and I felt myself drift away."

He described the sensations of going through a veil, into a calm peaceful corner where he was surrounded by euphoric sensations of warmth and love. He felt rapturous, and all of his usual inhibitions vanished. Eventually he remembered nothing.

"I swear, Mr. Dawson," He cried. "I can't remember anything after that—until I woke up in some other strange place next morning."

I woke up feeling numb, and I was certain that sometime during that night, something—"God Knows what"—had happened.

"A dead "reefer butt" was on the bed beside me, and my undershirt had a burn hole in it, and—and—Oh, Jeeesus!" He moaned. "—I knew I'd had sex with somebody, because my clothes and my underwear were all messed up." He cried.

"It scared me to death that I didn't know who I'd been with, and I was more scared because I couldn't tell anybody."

"Ronnie! That SOB, must 'a slipped me a 'Mickey' in that drink!" He wailed. "And I never smoked a reefer before.—but now I don't know!!!

Ya; think I did somethin'?" He blubbered. "Maybe—"Oh lord! I hope I didn't—maybe in the condition I was in, I did do something with Ronnie."

"Maybe he's always wanted to get something on me, 'cause maybe that way he gets back at my Dad for kicking him out of his pad." Cody ranted.

Ardro was beginning to feel Cody's anger. With effort, he said, "O.K. Cody, C'mon, try to get yourself together now. We're beginning to understand. We're gonna try to help you get this mess straightened out." Mr. Dawson nodded in agreement,

"But I didn't remember anything," Cody sobbed.

Next, he suddenly sat straight up. His demeanor changed completely

"But, then this!" He roared. "I do remember this part."

With several deep breaths he composed himself, and almost immediately, he continued his story.

"Two weeks later, I was so excited about getting ready for my wedding that I had almost completely forgotten that weird night on the town." "I had pushed it so far behind me." He sighed.

"Then one day I went to a travel agency, to make reservations for my honeymoon. I was looking for a credit card—one that I don't use very much—and when I found it; in behind that credit card there was something that really blew my mind."

"I nearly dropped the wallet when I realized what it was—"

He fell silent for a long time.

Mr. Dawson said gently, "Well Cody, what was it?

With total embarrassment, and a contorted face, he revealed:

"Ronnie had hidden one of his own pictures in my wallet." "And," distressfully he revealed, "On the back of it he had written—. He struggled to get it out. "—I can't say it, Mr. Dawson'"

Ardro realized at that moment, that other people—rich people—feel the same fears he's felt so often in his short lifetime.

'It's O.K. Cody" He encouraged. "You can say it to us. Go ahead, say it!"

"You really want to help me?" Queried Cody

"Yeah, we really do."

"Well . . ." Said Cody as he hesitantly pulled a plastic bag out of his shirt pocket, "Here." . . .

The bag contained the tattered picture that he nearly threw away. He had scrunched it up it in his hand, and then thought better of it. "I'll hold on to it." Then he put it in the bag, and hid it, thinking, "Nobody can ever see this."

They took the bag slowly from his hand, examined the picture, and agreed, "Humn, It's Ronnie Cook all right, lying beside what looks like you sleeping." And then they gasped, and glanced at each other when they turned it over.

Written on the back of it was: "Cody, that night was very special to me." And signed, "Your sweet Thang."

Ardro stifled a giggle, but a sharp jab of Mr. Dawson's elbow brought him back to the terrible nature of the situation for Cody. Cody sat with his head down as if in terrible pain.

Ardro, now controlled, spoke up. "O.K. Cody, What can we do? I know you tried to handle it by yourself, but it got outa hand. Right?

"Yeah, Right." Said Cody, with a rueful sigh. "But first let me explain something else."

"At first I didn't recognize the images, but it wasn't long before I realized that this could be used as evidence of something that would ruin my marriage—my future. And it would embarrass my family beyond repair."

"I got so sick that I almost 'threw-up'!"

"I went into a rage!"

So, on Sunday morning I found out where Ronnie lived. I know I shouldn't have—but I couldn't help it; I went straight to his house. He was there by himself. And when he saw me, he backed away, because he knew I was mad.

In my rage I showed him what I found in my wallet, and how I found it. "I was about ready to kill'im, right there." Seethed Cody. "And he knew it. He was scared, I know he was."

Then, Cody stood up to demonstrate. "I reached for him, and missed. I guess I must have relaxed a second.—That dude then snatched my wallet right out of my hand!"

Remembering that, Cody yelled. "Dammit!! Oh Man! I didn't expect that."

"But I was scared too," He cried. "Because I didn't want him, or anybody in the world, to have something that upsetting to my family and it's reputation."

He tried hard to make himself settle down.

"Well anyhow," He continued. "Ronnie, that Sorry Bastard, darted out of the house, and jumped into his car. I couldn't believe it, but . . . but . . . . He took off screaming, 'I'm gonna show it to everybody!'"

Oh, . . . "Noooh!" . . . I hollered. "I knew I couldn't let that happen. He might 'a had it in for my Daddy, but he couldn't do this to me."

"I took off too; in hot pursuit, but, in that car, he'd made a couple 'a fast turns, and I lost him. Shaking like a leaf, I was about ready to turn around."

"Then I spotted his car. Thank God, his gas was so low, that he had to stop at a Drive-up gas pump. I whirled into the station, and pulled up on the other side before he saw me. I ran around the corner, and when I saw him—wouldn't ya know it?—He had my wallet IN-HIS-HAND!"

"I came up on him from behind, caught him in a headlock, and—dumb me—since we were in a gas station, and people were looking, I even **asked** him to give me my wallet. I kept talking. I even told 'im it was a priceless family gift, and asked again." He just wouldn't turn it loose!"

"Pretty soon, I got tired of messing with him, and then I tried mightily to snatch it from him

"That dude's strong. Boy, he's strong!" Cody said excitedly, "I didn't realize how strong he was until . . . until I found my butt stretched out flat on the tarmac, and he was in his car flyin' away again."

"I was desperate then, God! Was I desperate!" he shrieked.

"So I took off again after him, and chased him cross town through the streets."

"Yeah, that's when I saw you chasing him, Cody." Ardro interrupted. "Ya'll were flyin'. When I got down to where I saw the police get in the chase, you'd disappeared. What happened then?"

"Well finally," he gulped, and took a deep breath. "I cornered him in a side street off 14th. He'd smashed into the side of somebody's truck, and that gave me a chance to jump out and grab' im again. I tackled and wrestled him for a minute, and tried to get my wallet out of his pocket. And then . . .—That damn fool stabbed me three times in my arm with his penknife!"

"Well, a few seconds later, the police came up and grabbed him; just as he was about to hit me with that knife again."

"To them, we were merely two black guys fighting. They just came up and grabbed us both"

"But when they looked around, and saw that it was Ronnie's car that smacked into that truck, he was in trouble then. So then I told them that he'd stolen my wallet; that's why I was chasing him. They took it from him, and in that instant, he gave me the wickedest grin."

"I coulda' smashed him, right there, but I got scared, and then I prayed to the Lord. "Please don't let 'em look in there."

"When they saw my I.D. they recognized my name, and didn't look any further. They handed the wallet to me."

"Man! What a relief! Those guys possibly saved my life."

"Then they arrested us both."

Cody sat back down, relieved that it was finally all out.

The street version of the story was exciting, but not as exciting as the real one, given by Cody. It seemed to be more logical; and certainly more important to Cody and his family. Mr. Dawson and Ardro assured Cody that they would try to find the answers and clear up the dreadful state of affairs.

Mr. Dawson advised. "You better get to a Doctor, Cody, right away. Ya' getting married ya' know . . . . Best you get tested for STD immediately."

Ardro added. "I sure hope you're O.K. Cody. Don't worry. We'll handle the story so that nobody in your family will be disgraced."

Mr. Dawson nodded his assurance. "You go home and relax, now."

Time flew by. Cody had spent over four hours with them. He left, feeling confident that he could go out and face the world again. Ardro was exhausted. It had been a long afternoon for him. He was "wound up!" He had shared in something awesome.

At about 4:00 o'clock, they left Mr. Dawson's "office," and went to his house. Ardro spent a relaxing half-hour with Liddy, before heading back to his own house. Liddy didn't question him, because she knew better than to talk about "their business;" her Daddy had taught her that a long time ago. And since he knew what he would meet when he got home, Ardro secretly wished that Helene had had the same training,

He did try to put Helene's questions off for the rest of the day, but she was ready for him. After a few pointed questions . . .

"Momma," He said tautly. "You already know almost all I know."

"You've heard all the neighborhood gossip, and most of it's pretty true, but now, I've got a lot more to do to really help Cody."

"Well what do you have to do?"

Ardro tried not to act annoyed. "Momma, I'm gonna help Mr. Dawson, and we're gonna get Cody out of his mess, you just watch."

"When that happens, I'll tell you a lot more. But not until then, O.K.?"

"All right, Honey, "She said, dejectedly. She was feeling left out again, but since she knew he was working with Mr. Dawson, it didn't worry her too much. "Just don't get all wound up in this stuff, and forget what you got to do, to get ready for college. She cautioned.

"Mom you know you don't have to worry about that," He declared as he walked out of the room. Jovially he waved. "And" wryly, "I Love You, Too." as he shut his bedroom door.

She heard his radio playing softly for only a few minutes, and then soon she knew he had gone to bed. He fell asleep quickly with his head filled with what he and Mr. Dawson and discussed after Cody left, that afternoon. As he dozed off, he was thinking, "I wanna be with Mr. Dawson at his lab when he examines that picture for evidence."

He and Mr. Dawson had agreed that they would work together the next afternoon. That made him so content he slept soundly.

Neither of them felt up to going to Church that Sunday morning. But even at home, Helene was still planning how to get people at the church involved with the kids. She vowed that she was going to talk to Pastor Kirkwood. "Maybe now, Ardro could work with some of those boys. He's learned a lot, this summer." She thought.

They spent the morning talking a lot about Ardro's future plans, and—much to his relief—avoided the thing about Cody. She did, however, mention pointedly that Mr. Mongus ought to offer some help to Ardro—even if to nobody else—because of what he's doing for Cody.

Early that afternoon, she strolled with him over to the Dawsons. He wanted to spend some time with Liddy before Mr. Dawson called him to duty.

Reluctantly leaving the "ladies" behind, they rode over to the lab. Although Ardro missed the chat with Liddy, he enjoyed the man-to-man link with Mr. Dawson. Mr. Dawson liked that too.

At the Lab, for the first time since Cody had showed it o them, they took the picture out, and they studied it. The rumples made it hard to examine, but they could see no more than what they had seen before.

Mr. Dawson then suggested that they look at it under his microscope. "There'll be fingerprints we might be able to use." He said. "And we don't know what else."

They studied it carefully, and then Mr. Dawson said, "Humn, Ardro look at this—real carefully."

Ardro had never been really been gung-ho about microscopes in school. He looked only when told to by the teacher. Now, at this moment, he was sorry that he had never really learned how to operate one. Little by little, with Mr. Dawson's instructions, he picked up the basics, and pretty soon, he was able to make sense out of what he saw.

It was a brand New World! He was fascinated. Under the scope Ardro noticed what looked like very faint chocolate brown streaks, and on top of them, hundreds of tiny shiny specks.

"What're those specks?"

"Don't know, Ardro, We'll have to check. But it's something." He sounded excited. "Something that doesn't belong on any picture." I'm going to take this to our chemists at the plant. They'll tell me.

As they took care of several details in the lab, Ardro said. "This kinda stuff is exciting, Mr. Dawson. We just might find out what really happened to Cody . . .—And this awesome microscope!" He exclaimed. "I gotta get back in school and learn all about this stuff!"

"You're on the right track, Ardro. Mr. Dawson said, heartily. In fact, I think we both are, in this case. If my guys identify this stuff, and if it's what I think it is, Cody's home free, and Ronnie's a dead duck!

"So, what do you think it is?" Asked a spellbound Ardro.

"Well," said Mr. Dawson thoughtfully, "you remember when Cody said, 'Ronnie Musta slipped me a Mickey.' Don't you?"

"Umm, Yes sir, I do." Said Ardro. "What's a Mickey—uh I mean—what's in it?"

"It's been a long time since I've seen or heard of one, but as I recall, it's not a nice concoction. Three things—none of them nice—are mixed together. Chicago gangsters used to use it in the 30's and 40's, to get control over people. It's a nasty brew. One of those chemicals is still used in the pharmaceutical business to help people. But in the wrong hands, it's awful." Explained Mr. Dawson.

I think that's what we saw through the microscope. It's called chloral hydrate—a nearly invisible white powder. The thugs would mix a tiny bit of that powder with raw alcohol, and water—in which they had soaked snuff."

"Snuff, what's snuff?" Asked Ardro.

Mr. Dawson chuckled. "Its ground-up tobacco, Ardro. Some real old people chew it,'n spit out the juice. You've seen that, I know. And you've probably seen some of the kids chew that brown stuff.—That's it."

"Ugh, Gross!"

"Yeah it is, but when it's all mixed together in another drink, it's tasteless.—And Potent. To tell you the truth, the drinker don't get a chance to taste it, because it induces distress, and in a few minutes he's in 'Never land.'"

"According to the doctors, chloral hydrate's a 'sedative-hypnotic, which causes disinhibition and euphoria.'"

"Huh? What's that mean?" Asked Ardro.

Mr. Dawson explained. "From what I can understand, it puts you in a trance where you feel in raptures. You sorta go out of your mind, and you do things you'd never do when you're O.K."

"Well that seems like what happened to Cody, don't it? Wow! That's almost worse than git'n Acid, like I did." Exclaimed Ardro

Mr. Dawson nodded. "We just have to wait to see if that's what happened."

* * *

X

Interlude

The next morning, Ardro went to school, and then stopped by the Counselor's office to see what courses he had to take in the fall. On the way home he applied for a couple of jobs. He got a lot of stuff done, but his mind was happily preoccupied with what he and Mr. Dawson had planned to do that afternoon.

While all this was going on, Helene was busily moving about the neighborhood, inquiring about possible jobs for Ardro during school, going to the school to find out about money for college, and talking to church people about "What was said in church yesterday about helping with the kids in the street?"

This was the only way she could keep her mind off the task that Ardro was doing, in addition to his schoolwork.

Her efforts were paying off too. She was surprised by a call from Pastor Kirkwood, soon after Cartel's funeral, that he got to thinking about the church trying to do something. Church officers were going to meet on the next Thursday night, and he asked her to come to the meeting.

She was stunned and happy by this happening, but at the same time, she thought, sarcastically.

"Money's what they're lookin' for."

She had also heard that other churches were talking about doing something too.

"Hope they don't fight among themselves. There's enough work out there to keep all of 'em all busy.—If they can get the money".

The Catholic Church is trying to get all the churches to come together, and start a recreation project.

"Humph! I don't think that'll ever happen"

With all these sarcastic feelings, she was at least getting people in the community to talk about all these proposals.

While downtown, she stopped by Mr. Mongus's office, just to talk for a minute with Mrs. Dawson. While they chatted, Mr. Mongus came out—and seeming extremely and strangely quiet—nodded, and vanished back into his office. They both knew he was embarrassed and uncomfortable, but they kept on talking. They talked about their kids, and without saying it, they showed that they hoped 'something good' would come out of their kids friendship.

They were proud and happy that things were turning out nicely.

That afternoon, Liddy and Ardro got their chance to walk down to the park. The lakeshore was crowded, but they found a place to sit where they could splash their feet in the water. It was the first time they could talk about personal things. All the other stuff had kept this in the background, but now that they were together without family or friends around, they felt free to begin to be sweethearts.

Just thinking about that possibility put Ardro's teeth on edge. He hesitantly slid up close to her, and then blurted out, "What do you think your Daddy's doing?"

She looked at him in agitated surprise. "I'm sorry? Ardro, why are you asking me about Daddy here?"

"Oh Lordy me!" He yelled in embarrassment. Liddy, I don't know why I said that! My brain, my heart and my mouth got all mixed up.

"I'm sorry. You make me all twittery."

She giggled. "Well at least, keep your **mind** on **me** for a change"

"O.K. Sure will." He grinned, took a deep breath, and suggested, "Let's go for a walk."

They strolled along—holding hands, and talked together for almost two hours. The afternoon was perfect, and they found that they had a lot more to talk about than History and school.

School did come up, however, near the end of the day. Now, as they discussed it, they both were thinking about where they wanted to go to college. And they realized that they didn't want to be too far away from each other.

Also, Ardro had never given much thought to the cost of college. He never dreamed that it costs so much. When Liddy told him of all the concerns her parents had talked about; such things as tuition and all the other fees, he felt kind 'a sick.

"Does Momma know all this?" He wondered silently, with a sinking feeling.

Liddy was unaware of his concerns, and she kept right on talking about buying clothes and curtains for her room, and on, and on—.

When she noticed that he had become unusually quiet,

"What's the matter, Ardro? Don't you want me to go away?"

"Oh Liddy." He sighed. "That's not what I was thinking. I want you to go ahead and do what you have to do."

"It's me I'm thinking about." He fretted. "I want to do the same thing, but God knows, I don't see how me and Momma's gonna do it."

Liddy squeezed his hand, with helpless understanding.

Then he brightened. "Ya know, Liddy." ". . . Well, now I'm gonna talk about your Daddy again. And this time I mean to. You know he's been helping me to find a way to help Cody. Wouldn't it be great if we do help 'im, then maybe—just maybe—Mr. Mongus might want to find a way to help me?"

"Yes Ardro," She agreed, and seemed pleased at the thought. "Maybe so. I hope so."

At that time, it was nearing five o'clock, quitting time, and Mr., Dawson was busy at this desk when his office phone rang. He was summoned to the Chemistry research department. His report was ready.

He closed down quickly, and rushed over to the laboratory testing-center. Although it was time to go home, the lab techs carefully and thoroughly explained their procedures, before they showed him the results. He was extremely satisfied.

They had found multiple fingerprints, and they even revealed that the picture became contaminated with the stuff while it was inside a pocket. They could see lint from that pocket, on the picture.

They told him that, what Ardro and he had come across was, something that was rare at that time—the combination of Chloral Hydrate, snuff and alcohol. "Some time ago, that combo was used for a Mickey Finn—but not much any more. There's a lot more new stuff out there nowadays. Still, whoever gets that kind'a Mickey is in real trouble."

"Hope the Dude that made it hasn't showed anybody else how to do it.

Go get'im, Dawson," urged one of the men.

Mr. Dawson assured them, that the guy is, "in my sights."

They relaxed, and before they left, started joking around. One of them wisecracked, "Good looking dude, Dawson.—Funny note on the back.—Somebody you know?"

He quipped back. "I can arrange for you to meet him tomorrow, if ya wanna."

Their laughter was silly fun.

Mr. Dawson thanked them for their hard work. Then he left the genial banter, "You guys are almost better then the city crime lab." He beamed He was happy.

Ardro and Liddy were just walking up when he pulled into the driveway. He smiled to himself at the way they looked together. They looked serious, but he could tell that they enjoyed each other.

When they noticed him, they both hurried to meet him, and Ardro immediately asked the question. "Found out anything yet, Mr. Dawson?"

"Yeah," He said noncommittally, "I'll fill you in, in a few minutes. Nothing you can do tonight, but you've got a busy day tomorrow."

After they all had greeted Mrs. Dawson, He and Mr. Dawson sat together, while he shared what he had found out.

Ardro was happy, and satisfied, and scared—all at the same time.

"Now, what are we gonna do, Mr. Dawson?

"Not we" emphasized Mr. Dawson, "You!

"Omigod! **Me**? By myself?" He panted—keenly anxious—and he eagerly asked. "How, Mr. Dawson?"

"Well Ardro, you've learned to use tricks. What you have to learn to do now is think and plan—Use your head."

"Right now," He ordered. "Think! Ardro, think about what you ought to do with this information.

After a silent minute, Ardro said, "Well, I guess I ought to keep it quiet—at least 'til first thing in the morning."

"Now you're thinking. What are you going to do with it in the morning?"

"Uh, uh . . . . Call the police, and then have'em call you." He said unsurely.

Mr. Dawson chuckled. "Well O.K. Ardro."

He reasoned. "At least they'll know the report came from you. I suppose they'll have to know how you got the information, and I'll let them know what happened."

They parted.

Ardro's day—Courting Liddy, and accomplishing something so fantastic—couldn't have been more wonderful. Both were things beyond his wildest dreams.

When he got home, his eyes were bright with tears. Alarmed, Helene rushed to him, but as soon as she embraced him, she realized that these were tears of happiness and relief. She didn't know why, but she was near tears right along with him. Their joy was magic.

* * *

XI

The Payoff

The next day Ardro did most of his homework at school, then dashed home to let Helene know that he was on an errand for Mr. Dawson.

He approached the police station about 3:30, glancing around to make absolutely sure that he was unobserved when he went in. He was concerned that if somebody saw him, very few of his buddies would ever trust him again. After another quick look all up and down the street, he darted through the door. It was kind of dim in there, but he saw a lighted window, and went directly to it—the office. The secretary, startled by his sudden appearance, called an on-duty officer, who hurried to the open window.

Without a pause, he loudly announced. "My name is Ardro Knight, and I want to talk, privately with a patrolman, about something I've seen."

They looked at each other, and shrugged. The secretary nodded toward the officer. "Mr. Potts is here, if you want to talk to him."

"Yes," said Ardro, "I'll talk to him if he knows about what's going on in the streets.

"That, I do Ardro." Said Mr. Potts quickly. He stiffly invited, him to "Come on back," as he unlocked the door.

Ardro could feel his hair moving. He'd never been inside a police station before. He jumped when he heard the door lock click behind him, and wondered what his school buddies would think, if they saw him there.

This must have been visible on his face, because Mr. Potts chuckled. He imagined what Ardro was feeling. "Ardro," if you haven't done anything bad, you don't have to worry. You're O.K. here.

"O.K. Sir." said Ardro shakily. And thinking that someone might come in and recognize him, "Uh, can we get over to the side, a little bit?"

As they moved to a far corner, out of the line of sight, the officer relaxed and became friendlier, and Ardro thought, "Now he seems almost human."

"Well what's the story? Ardro." Mr. Potts asked casually.

"Well, Mr. Potts," He started nervously. "I saw something I wanna talk about." And he continued with the story about watching the car chase on last Sunday, about the wreck, about Cody getting stabbed and about the arrest of the two men.

Mr. Potts was intent. "Yes, Ardro. I remember hearing some of the officers talking about that. One of the fellows was Mr. Mongus' boy, right?

"Yeah, you're right. He's the one that got stabbed. And there's a whole lot more to the story".

While Mr. Potts listened, Ardro continued.

"You know a Mr. Dawson, don't you? He works for NCB.

"Sure, I know him. I see him around town a lot.

Well, he's a friend,—Uh, I'm one of his daughter's friends.—And I get a chance to talk to him a lot. He knows I get along good with my bunch of friends on the street, and I can talk to them. Se he showed me how to get to the real facts about what I just told you. And I found out something.

"Yes, go on, what is it, Ardro?

"Oh, I can't tell you that yet," Hung back Ardro, "but Mr. Dawson can. And he wants somebody from here that knows him, to call him. He'll give you all the information you need to help solve a problem for everybody—especially for Cody Mongus. I know Mr. Mongus will be happy about that."

With a slightly frustrated look, Mr. Potts leaned back, sighed and said, "O.K. Ardro, I know him and he knows me. I'll call him right now. Maybe he can come over right away.

While he was waiting for someone to answer the phone, he asked. "You want to wait and see? We're all working on it, and since you know so much, maybe you can help more."

"Humm! Can I?" In his wildest dreams, Ardro never thought a cop would invite him to sit in on a conversation with someone else. He was giddy with delight.

Nobody answered the phone, but Mr. Potts asked for a quick return call.

While they waited, Ardro continued.

"Yeah. Mr. Dawson'll tell you all the stuff we found. We've been working on it together."

"Well, if what you've came up with helps us, it sounds like you two have done this Cody fellow a great big favor.

"That's why I wanna be a cop—a undercover cop. I really wanna be a cop." He felt himself getting fired-up. "I wanna help people. There's all kinds of stuff goin' on out there in the street that's makin' it bad for kids in school, and I want to help root it out, and kill it."

"Huh! So you really want to be a cop? I never heard a kid, like you, talk like that before." Said Mr. Potts.

"Uh, whatdya mean, 'a kid like me', Mr. Potts?

With an uneasy sway, "Well . . . uh . . . I'm talking about Black kids—Black boys, especially"

"Yeah," Ardro quietly and thoughtfully agreed. "I guess you're right. Most of 'em hate cops." And for the first time, he looked Mr. Potts straight in the eye. "—Or are scared of them. Cops chase 'em all the time, and then put 'em in jail. Cops don't care about 'em. No friends there."

Mr. Potts nodded in understanding.

"Well, when I'm a cop," Ardro continued. "I wanna care about 'em. I want to be a friend to the good ones, and get the really bad ones off the streets.

The phone ringing, interrupted them.

"It's Mr. Dawson." Called the secretary.

"Hi, Jim, Thanks for calling back." Said Mr. Potts. "Your friend, Ardro is here. "He's told me a lot of stuff about the Mongus boy's trouble, and he tells me that you know a whole lot more. Can you come over?"

As Mr. Potts talked, Ardro's ears pricked up. He thought, "Jim?—I didn't know Mr. Dawson's name was Jim." He was flabbergasted that Mr. Dawson was "in" with the police that well. He found himself wondering whether they knew as much about Mr. Dawson as he knew. "Nah, Probably not." He told himself.

Anyhow, he was relieved to hear that Mr. Dawson was on his way over. "I won't be in this by myself for long now." He thought.

While they waited, he felt strangely at ease, and continued sharing his feelings about being a cop.

Fervently, he said, "I wish all cops could be friends to kids. They'd get a lot more done."

"You'll find out when you get there Ardro," said Mr. Potts, defensively, "that its not that easy,"

Then he changed the subject. "Where're you planning to go to school?"

"Well, I'm planning to graduate from High School next spring. Then I have to find a school—a college—that'll teach me all about police work, and that's gonna take money.

"Humn," And as a compliment, "You seem older than that. I sure hope you make it, Ardro."

"Thanks!" Then Ardro added. "Ya know? I never heard a cop—like you—talk like that before."

Mr. Potts got the point. He chuckled. He appreciated the compliment.

At that moment, Mr. Dawson rushed through the door. "O.K. Guys," He said briskly, "I've got a 4:30 engagement. Let's get it over."

"Whoa, Jim! Not so fast. There's a whole lot we got to get out today."

Mr. Dawson turned, looked over at Ardro, and winked. "Well, Ardro can tell you almost as much as I can. After I hand over the basics, he can fill you in on all the details you want. "He's the man," He said, pointing meaningfully to Ardro.

Ardro's heart pounded, during this whirlwind exchange, and felt nearly overwhelmed with what had been thrown into his lap.

Now it was time for his Big Move!

He forced himself to sit calm and collected, while Mr. Dawson explained the legal stuff about the controlled substance, Chloral Hydrate; how it was used in a Mickey, and how it was used in an assault against Cody. He told why Cody reacted irrationally the way he did. And finally, he gave all the legal reasons why Ronnie Cook should immediately be arrested.

When he finished, he looked around and said, "Now, I've got to go. Ardro's got all the rest."

With that, Mr. Dawson hurried out the door, leaving Mr. Potts very impressed, and Ardro in a state of panicky euphoria. "I'm in charge now?" He wondered.

Mr. Potts interrupted his thoughts. "O.K. Ardro, "We're in charge now—You and me!" Yep, Now you know. I've been working on this thing, almost by myself, from the start. I'm sure glad you came in, and I'm sure glad you're here now."

Ardro's happy nervous tension made him almost scream.

"My first case! And I ain't even a cop yet." He silently chanted. "I helped somebody. I'm gonna get Cody out of a pickle." He even dared to think that this might be a way to get Mr. Mongus to think he was worth something—somebody he might help get an education.

Again Mr. Potts called him back to reality. "Come on, Ardro. Give me the rest." He urged.

After a short pause to settle himself down, Ardro related the rest of the story to Mr. Potts. He described all the details; how they found them out, how they tested them, and who was responsible. It took nearly twenty minutes, but by the time he had finished, Mr. Potts was satisfied that all the bases had been covered.

When Ardro finished, Mr. Potts grinned, extended his hand, and said heartily, "Good job, Ardro. Pretty soon they'll be calling you Detective Knight."

That thought jolted Ardro's senses like a bombshell. He jumped up, and asked quickly, "Where's the bathroom?"

There, in the bathroom, all these new possibilities swept him away. And again, uncontrolled tremors of pride and joy rippled like a river.

In three days, the police had tracked down Ronnie in a small town 47 miles away. He claimed he had gone to visit his grandmother. From his jail cell, he claimed that he had done nothing wrong, and . . . "I'll get even."

When the police called Cody. Naturally, he didn't want the full story made public. But they did want him to help them decide the charges that ought to be brought against Ronnie.

Since it would destroy him if his parents, or fiancée knew it all. He agreed that they charge Ronnie with aggravated assault, and communicating threats. He suggested that they give him a long probation, and explicitly urged that there would an endless restraining order, protecting anyone in the Mongus family.

When Cody met with Ardro and Mr. Dawson, he was almost wordless with delight and gratitude. They had, in a very real sense, saved his life.

"And Ardro," He grabbed him in a heartfelt bear hug. "I've heard my brother talk about you, but I never knew you before"

"Now you're my angel. And I'll never forget it!

With dignity, Ardro said, "And I wish you the best, Cody."

"Well Ardro," Continued Cody. My Daddy doesn't know all the dirty details—I hope he never does—but he's going to know about what you've done for me. This'll help him find out, that a lot of the guys he been calling "gutter-rats" have good sense, and spunk, and get-up-and-go." What they have always needed is somebody to support them."

"He's gotta do something for them, Ardro, and especially for you, because without you—and what 'pull' he's got—he would have put me in the same boat."

Mr. Dawson interrupted to agree. "Your Daddy's 'pull' got you out of jail, Cody" "And now that 'pull' can be a terrific help in this community to get something started for our young people—to help them get some of that support."

"Well, now, he's gotta do it!" Stressed Cody. "What you and Ardro have done, has helped him to 'save face,' and when I'm done talking to him, I'm pretty sure he'll want to make a big show of his gratitude."

—And with a hearty chuckle—Cody added, "and make a bigger show of his newfound generosity of spirit."

* * *

XII

Predicted Dreams

Mr. Mongus' plan evolved out of thankfulness—thankfulness for the restoration of his, and his family's reputation. Also, it gave him a chance to demonstrate his change of heart. It was, in fact, his chance to make a comeback but, as Cody predicted, it turned into a dazzling show.

He involved the mayor, the chief of police, his friends and other community dignitaries in his plan—his plan to change his image in the city.

One of the main functions of this group that he created was to sponsor a college scholarship fund, which was intended to help kids in the neighborhood whose parents had rented one of his properties.

Mr. Mongus was happy for their cooperation, and to his satisfaction, everyone in the group supported his very impressive plan. There were additions, amendments and adjustments, but he had achieved a positive leadership role in the community. He had loosened up, and he enjoyed it.

Helene's telephone rang. It was Mrs. Dawson calling from Mr. Mongus' office; and her voice held a strange sense of excitement. She didn't give any details but made an appointment for them, for 3:30 p.m. the next day because Mr. Mongus wanted to talk with her about Ardro.

Helene hadn't heard the scholarship declaration, but she too, tingled with anticipation.

"Oh! Oh yes, Mrs. Dawson. I'll meet him at school, and we'll be there. Thank You," She pealed.

He was glumly on his way home when he saw Helene coming to meet him. It had been a tough day. Since he had been busy the night before—doing what he believed he had to do for Cody, he hadn't done his schoolwork well. He was out of sorts.

"Oh, Good Lord, Momma! What a ya doin' here? What's up?

She started grinning. "Ardro, Mr. Mongus wants to see us at 3:30—Today!!"

"Ya' know why, Momma?" He was a little agitated.

"Nope, I don't, but I can guess. Can't you?"

His gloom vanished. "And I didn't even get a chance to wash my face," He grinned.

"Here, I brought along a wet wash rag. Do it now." She cheerily ordered.

After a quick sandwich, they set off to Mr. Mongus office.

Mrs. Dawson's greeted them warmly, and they were filled with anticipation, as they waited for Mr. Mongus to come out. Helene jovially whispered half-aloud. "Maybe, if the ol' goat won't give ya any money, he's got a good job for ya—He oughta!"

Mrs. Dawson overheard her, and smiled.

At that time Mr. Mongus made his appearance. He was not pretentious at all. Surprisingly, in fact Helene had never seen him with such a look of contrite kindness.

After their cordial greetings, the first thing he said was, "I'm sorry, Mrs. Knight. I apologize"

Helene's mouth fell open. Half sarcastically she asked. "For what, Mr. Mongus?"

"First of all," Uh . . . He hesitated; trying to find his words, "for the way I talked to you when you came in about your boy."

"And secondly," He continued with difficulty. "For my haughty mind-set, about our black kids . . . . You see, Ms. Knight, uh, I've been trying to protect my own kids. And because of that, I've put the wrong labels on a lot of others." He said ruefully, "It's been a bad call."

Helene nodded in total agreement. Then she said, "Well, Mr. Mongus I'm sorry about that too, 'cause there's a lotta good kids out there."

"I know. I know that now." Conceded Mr. Mongus. "And, You've got one, right here."

Helene sparkled at that.

Mr. Mongus then gently placed his hand on Ardro's shoulder, and said, more kindly than Helene had ever heard him speak, "Ardro, what you have done, has meant immeasurably more to my family than you'll ever know. Thank you. I didn't realize that a young man like you could become such a success."

Ardro' heart leaped. Almost overcome, he stammered, "Uh . . . I did what I most wanted to do, Mr. Mongus. Uh . . . I'm glad it helped."

Mr. Mongus looked at Ardro, and shook his head gratefully, then turned again to Helene, "I understand, Mrs. Knight, that Ardro wants to keep on doing police work." He boomed. "That's exciting! That's important! That's the kind of career he can be great in." And then he crooned. "I want to help him!"

"Oh, Thank you, Mr. Mongus." She gushed. "I know he'll do a good job at whatever you give him to do."

"I don't want to give him a job, Mrs. Knight. He's done a good job already. Now he needs to finish school—get prepared—and get equipped to keep on doing it."

"Yes??"

He pulled himself up to his old prideful self, and announced:

"Well to begin with, Mrs. Knight, I'm about to tell you and Ardro something that is not to be announced publicly until all the details have been settled. However, I want you two to be the first to know."

Grandiosely, he revealed. "I've been meeting with the Mayor, some preachers, The BPOA (Black Police Officers Association) and some other important folks. Together we've come up with a plan that may help many of the Black boys in our community."

"Humn!" Breathed a delighted Helene. "Oh, that's so good!" She chirruped, as she glanced at Ardro. "They sure need it, Mr. Mongus."

With his hand on Ardro's shoulder again, Mr. Mongus then said directly to him. "And starting with you, Ardro—You will be the first.—And then every year from next year on, some boy whose family has rented from me will receive a scholarship from Mongus, Inc., to go to college.

"And Ardro, because of what you've done, you will get two full years." Ardro groaned with delight.

"You'll earn it, because I'm asking you to work along with us to select the others. Think you can do that?"

"I'll sure try, Mr. Mongus. I'll do the best I can." Assured Ardro.

"That's good enough." Said Mr. Mongus as he pompously strode across the room, continuing to talk. "On top of that, we're going to create some kind of community venture, or association, that's going to pull together every community agency with the churches and schools. It's a big project—a dream, but I think it can be done."

"Also Ardro, since the BPOA has heard about what you want to do for a career, they're going to start talking to the school people about working with kids in the neighborhood to make them feel better about cops, and how they can help improve community."

With that, Mr. Mongus sat down heavily, as if he'd just finished a lecture.

Helen said in awe and thanksgiving. "You've done all that, Mr. Mongus?"

"That's not enough, Ms. Knight. I didn't realize it until Ardro proved to me a point that I've been missing all these years; that so many of the kids in this community have real value. They just need more attention."

Ardro almost fainted, and Helene let out an unladylike whoop. "Oh, My God, Mr. Mongus, God Bless You!!!" She cried.

Ardro, still speechless, sidled over to a chair. "Thank you, Mr. Mongus." He said, barely above a whisper.

Mr. Mongus slowly emerged from his somber, businesslike attitude. He suddenly and brightly announced grandly, "And Ardro. if you still want'em," I'm going to buy you a brand new pair of high class Roller Blades."

That broke the tension. They all laughed with gusto.

Mrs. Dawson heard the merriment in the office, and she breathed a sigh of happiness for all of them. She knew that they all were happy once more.

She could hardly wait to get home and tell Jim.

Through a thunderous summer storm, Helene and Ardro strolled home arm in arm—Helene loudly humming an old hymn, "I Am Washed By The Blood Of The Lamb, "and Ardro enjoying the feeling of cool water washing away his troubles.

Ardro's first thoughts when they left the office were about Liddy. He wanted to be the first one to tell her about his good fortune. Of course he didn't reckon with Helene's dash to the telephone at home.

"Momma" he cautioned. "Remember what Mr. Mongus said about blabbing it before it comes out in the Newspaper."

"Um, yeah, But I gotta tell Tina."

"Yeah, and I gotta tell Liddy too." He grinned. "I'm going over there now, if it's O.K. I want to get there before her Mom or Dad gets a chance to tell her. But let's not tell everybody else yet, O.K.?"

"O.K." She grinned. "Now you hurry back," She yelled, as he dashed out into the rain again.

Liddy couldn't imagine who was on their back porch at the door. She hardly recognized Ardro. When she did, she unlocked and opened the door.

"Ardro, what's wrong?" She asked in alarm. "Why are you out in this rain—no coat or anything?"

"Oh, Liddy, nothings wrong." He said excitedly. "I've got good news, that's all. And I wanted to tell you first, before anybody else did. Your Mom and Dad know, but they haven't told you."

"O.K. Ardro, Settle down." She coaxed. "You're soaking wet. Here, sit down." And she led him to a settee on the porch. "Tell me. What news is so good that you had to run here through a thunderstorm?

"I'm gettin' to go to college, Liddy." He announced. His eyes glistened with happiness. "The Lord, Mr. Mongus and your Daddy have made it possible."

She squealed "Oh Ardro, that's fantastic!" as she leaned to hug him, but she immediately drew back. He was wet as a duck.

He grinned. "That's O.K."

They hadn't even heard Mr. Dawson drive up, but at that moment, he darted through the door out of the rain.

He grinned from ear to ear. "My God, boy! What happened to you? Did you swim over here?

Ardro just then became fully aware that he was wringing wet.

With a chill, Ardro Sniggered "No, Mr. Dawson, I just couldn't wait to get over here to tell Liddy."

"Well, let me get you a dry shirt, M' boy, and then we can all bring each other up to date."

Mrs. Dawson came in at the same time, and joined them from the front. She was not at all surprised to find him there. They were both, full of congratulations.

It was a joyful evening. Mr. Dawson helped Ardro fill in the details of the whole proposition.

"I was there with about eleven people. Cody was one of them."

Then he was careful to add that, "Even the Social Services people were anxious to find out how they could best advise people."

"And he pointed out that, of course, most of the basic money is coming from Mr. Mongus' business corporation".

Mrs. Dawson chimed in to say, "Mr. Mongus is really happy over this. Most people, along with me, never recognized that there is, in reality, a nice guy underneath. Ya' know, He's really kind of shy."

"Wow!" Said Ardro in awe. "He sure had a lotta people scared of 'im." "Some people, like Momma, almost hated 'im."

"Yes," Mrs. Dawson smiled quietly. "I certainly understand. He **is** hard to work for, but I know, that he was that way in order to seem businesslike to the public. And, to have enough clout to make certain the rents were paid, he purposely developed, and practiced that style. And most of the time it worked too."

"Thanks, Mrs. Dawson." Said Ardro. "Now I know where that weird urge to help Cody and Mr. Mongus came from."

"Well, he can't change too much yet." Grinned Mr. Dawson

"But Ardro," He continued. You've helped him become aware that his attitude was bad for the community. And now, he is delighted to get this chance to change it. Actually, that change has caused other business people to cooperate, and work to contribute to the fund. And I hope this works too."

Ardro glowed inside, and enjoyed the delicious feeling of Liddy squeezing his hand. She dreamed of what could be possible in the future, and now she knew that she wanted him to be successful.

Through it all—with Liddy by his side, Ardro was euphoric. And his euphoria was enhanced by thoughts of Squeaky, and possibly of Odell. "Maybe now, they can be hopeful enough to go back to school."

On the other hand, he was saddened by thoughts of the waste of Cartel, and Shacky, and the others.

"God!" He thought, "It would be great if this was the final fix."

It was however, a great beginning in that community.

Just then, Beautiful red rays from the late evening sun flashed through the trees. "Oh, I wish Momma was here. She knows most of this, but she would love to be here now with you all. It seems like the storm's all gone for all of us, and the sun is shining. I'm so happy. Thank you!"

He looked at Liddy, and wanted to kiss her, then thought better of it at that moment. She knew what he was thinking, and smiled—looking more beautiful than he had ever seen her. Her parents chuckled, glanced at each other and excused themselves.

On his was out, Mr. Dawson said, "Ardro, I know you're trying to get some extra money for school this year. I think I can find some leads for you. Don't worry. All you have to do is . . . your very best in school. You'll always have a way to earn to extra the money you'll need while you're in college too.

This was music to Ardro's ears. "I'm so glad I know you folks, and I'll always appreciate you. Thanks"

This time, he was high, only on joy. It seemed, as in a dream, that no time elapsed before he was at home with Helene.

Dinner was especially delicious. Helene couldn't ask many questions, because she knew most of the answers, but she filled his ears with the responses she had received from the friends she had shared the news with.

In fact, Pastor Kirkwood surprised Helene.

"You know, That preacher never called me before, but now since he heard that Mr. Mongus wants to help, he called to see if Tina, I, and several of the other church people would come to a meeting to talk about what the church could do."

"Yeah, He's real interested now, especially since there might be some money for the church in it." She declared. "They sure need it."

That, and a lot more conversation filled the rest of the evening.

For the first time Ardro felt relaxed. He talked with Helene about his growing relationship with Liddy.

"Ya Know, Momma," Ardro rambled. "It's funny how things change." After a long considerate pause, he continued. "Everything changed, when I made up my mind to change. Just think. When I decided to go back to school, I met Liddy. Then, I met Mr. and Mrs. Dawson, and—and . . ." He struggled to express himself.

"And, if I'd 'a kept on messin' up, I wouldn't 'a come out the way I did.

"Now look at me Momma." He crowed, "I'm goin' to college!" "If I hadn't changed, all these doorways wouldn't have opened up.

"Yeah, Ardro," crooned Helene. "Ya' growin' up fast.

"Sometimes I think, too fast, Momma. But maybe it's just 'cause I'm catching up".

"School's important to me now. One more year!" He rejoiced. "And I'll be going to college. Boy, I sure wish Liddy were going too. She is; but at another school."

"How you like her, Mom?"

"Why?" She grinned.

"Oh Momma, it ain't gonna be like that. We're real good friends, and we gotta keep it that way, at least 'til we're out of' school."

"Keep it that way." She admonished. "This is going to be a busy school year for us all. None of us has got time to be foolin' around. I'm gonna be working down at the church with the committee, and tryin' to keep things together here. You can't slack off, Ardro. You gotta qualify for that college scholarship, and go to that police school.

"Not just a police school, Momma. Now, I'm getting' a real college degree."

Delight and determination was back in their lives.

* * *

XIII

The Finals

Ardro eagerly started his Senior year with high expectations. Just before school began, he had had a long talk with his old friend, "Squeaky," Lacey Rogers, who was no longer "Squeaky" to most of the kids now—he was Lacey. His old squeaky sneakers had worn out long ago, but he did allow Ardro an occasional, jovial "Squeaky." Ardro was glad that he had successfully convinced "Squeaky"—uh Lacey—to try a placement test. Not surprisingly, he took the test, and passed it with flying colors. That first semester back, he enrolled in school for half a day, just to brush up on being in a classroom. Ardro was almost sorry that he was back, because just keeping up with the rest of the class was a challenge, and after unsuccessfully trying to keep up with Lacey, he consoled himself, "That's O.K. He's smarter then me.

Although Ardro wanted to prove that he was a top-notch student, his first intent was to undo all the ills his mistakes had caused. And in order to do that, from then on he worked tirelessly—not caring what his peers thought about him, or how he was leaving them, their fears and their threats behind. For the first time in his life he just wanted to prove that he could compete with the best. Lacey and Liddy kept him inspired, and kept his nose to the grindstone. They both helped him set his own standards. And he was happy that Lacey was there. "Squeak being here will make me keep my standards high." He thought.

Several of his other buddies, including Hugh, were back. And together, they all anticipated a happy year. Although Hugh was still in 11th grade, he now became even more friendly and open with Ardro. Hugh now seemed especially at-ease in school with Ardro's friends, and associated easily with all kinds of students. For the first time, he seemed to be really enjoying new acquaintances.

When Ardro shared this fact with Helene, she chuckled, and said. "Mr. Mongus musta really changed".

As the year progressed, Ardro and Liddy became even closer. His visits with her were no longer just study sessions, and their parents were cautiously accepting of the relationship. Together these families had experienced some trying times, and so they worked together to avoid any other complications.

Out of that, and out of that mutual interest in their kids, grew a very strong supportive bond. Ardro was beginning to experience a feeling that he had missed when he was a kid—the feeling of "family." He found himself thinking more and more about his daddy—wishing that he and Helene could be like Mr. & Mrs. Dawson. At that time he didn't even know where his Daddy was, but he vowed that when he graduated, he was going to contact him.

No school year is perfect. Not surprisingly, during Ardro's senior year there were several irritations. One happened as he and Liddy were walking up the stairway to another class. He overheard a comment "Here 'e comes."—Followed by a giggling question—"Who d'ya think ya are . . . a 'Black Baby Einstein'?"

Some of the other ne'er-do—well timewasters were loafing there, and started harassing him because he was doing so well in school. Among them, someone yelled, Yo, Nerdy-Birdy! . . . Ya better watch ya back, Smarty Show-off, or we'll whup it!"

He felt Liddy's yank on his shirtsleeve. "C'mon Ardro," She urged. He cast a threatening glance at the dudes, but even though it shook him a little, he took it in stride, resolutely ignoring their jibes. He was thankful that he she was with him.

Only one really shocking event marred the rest of the year.

The entire school was disrupted most of one morning. One whole class period was completely ruined. Archie, his impudent mouthy summer school classmate in his Algebra class, had made a bad mistake. He spit out a one-too-many off-color comment to Donna Royce—one of the girls in school. Ardro heard one of the onlookers say, "What he said to her musta wiped her out, because it sure set her off. She put him in the hospital with a very nasty wound in his butt, which she viciously inflicted with a long sharp pair of scissors.

Mr. Browne was pale with excitement and exhaustion. "Glad I'm not going to be a principal." Ardro thought.

Both he and Liddy were able to get through that day. Fortunately nothing this serious happened again that year.

Archie's wounds were serious, and his hospital stay was unfortunately long. Donna went to juvenile court, and her experience in juvenile detention was similar to Ardro's—only longer. Because of this episode, they both missed so much school that neither of them was able to make the grades to pass the semester.

One positive outcome of this unpleasant incident was, that during the initial investigation, several policemen from the BPOA began to circulate throughout the school. Their presence was positive, and they began to have conversations with the kids about proper conduct, and self-protection while in school. They even had occasional lunches in the cafeteria. The result was that the kids were no longer leery in their presence. In fact, they were pretty impressed.

On their leisurely walk home one day, he told Liddy, "Hope they keep coming back. I'd like to get a chance to say something to some of 'em.

"Yeah, I'm sure you will, Ardro.

They walked along in comfortable silence for a while, and then he spoke up again.

"It keeps buggin' me Liddy." He was almost sad. He knew that there was a good chance that Archie would never come back. "I didn't like 'im, but he's smart and he could do a lot in this world, if he learned to control his big mouth." And, thinking about Uncle Berty, he wondered. "Did Uncle Berty's mouth get him in the same kind of trouble?"

"It's that kind of dumb stuff that stops the guys." For the first time in his life, he asked himself, "What happened that my daddy didn't stay in school?"

Determined, now more than ever. He vowed, "This is not going to happen to me."

"I've got a pretty good idea of what happened to Uncle Berty, but Daddy's a mystery. It's too late for them, but it's not too late for my little buddies." He vowed. "After I'm graduated, I'm sure gonna help to make things different."

On the way home that day Liddy learned a whole lot about what was driving him; and they discussed that.

"I know you mean it, Ardro, and I know you'll find a way." She comforted. "Being a good police undercover man will be a good start. But it's hard, Ardro. You see what my Daddy goes through. I hope you'll be happy, Ardro." She said earnestly. And she added, teasingly, "I just might do something in college that will fit right in."

"He stopped dead still, looked at her with all the love he could muster, and said delightedly, "Liddy . . . together we'd make a big splash. We'd be swimmin' in seventh heaven."

His love, his successful hard work and a series of exciting events made the rest of the summer fly by. In retrospect, he thought he'd never make it.

During that year, he often told Mr. Dawson how grateful he was to Liddy, the Dawson family and the BPOA. Liddy's love, Helene's support, and their helping to get the money to buy his books and all his supplies made him feel happier than he had been in months. He never said it out loud, but he was glad that he didn't have to have a job, and could spend all his time on his schoolwork—and of course do a little courting. Helene was just as happy, because she was busily making contacts, drumming up community activities, and this getting help for others like him.

This spell of happiness caused him to ruefully remember several of his friends who had gone astray.

Archie, the loudmouth agitator; though he eventually got out of the hospital, never came back to school. The stab wound took its toll. His basketball days were over. Unfortunately, that was his only real attraction to school. So he dropped out—unable to do work that required him to lift much weight.

He still had "the mouth" though. The snide reflection, "That oughta get him somethin' besides killed," tickled Ardro. He really felt bad for Archie. He even considered "I think he's a pretty smart dude too. Maybe, If I'd known him better, we coulda been friends."

Donna, the girl that stabbed Archie, never showed up again either.

"She was in the Juvenile detention center with me." One of the girls at school reported. "I only saw her for a about a week, then they moved her down to the end of the hall where they pinned her up by herself. She musta gone really crazy. Poor thing."

These recurring thoughts only spurred Ardro on to his own success.

During the Christmas Holidays, he and Helene went—at the invitation of the Dawsons—out with the family to dinner. There, they again became engaged in a long conversation, about the fate of kids that are not now in their class. The regretful recollection of Archie and Donna—These two, along with Shack, Cartel and a long list of others not back in school, were discussed In the course of these moments in the conversation, someone tapped Ardro on the shoulder from behind. He turned around.

"Michael!" Ardro yelped, and leaped up happily. "You old goat, I thought you left town."

After the hearty embrace, they were all surprised to see Michael—one of Ardro's cohorts in 'the attack'.

"Yeah Ardro." He grinned, "They pinned me down. I didn't want to, but they sent me to the Juvenile Detention Center for three months. Got out too late to make summer school. But, now I'm going to a private school, the Hollyville Academy."

"Hollyville Academy? Hollyville?" Helen piped up. "I didn't know about a private school there in Hollyville."

"Michael, that's the town where my Uncle Berty lives, said Ardro. Remember I used to talk about him?"

"Humn—, Yeah Ardro, I just might look 'im up" Buzzed Michael.

Helene smiled pleasantly at the reunion.

They chatted pleasantly about this, and other things, for a few more minutes before Michael went back to a table with his family.

As Michael walked away, Ardro looked at Helene, and said forthrightly, "Ya know Momma, I'm kinda glad we had it rough.

Her sidelong glance told him to continue, but then she considered. "Yes Ardro, but we've had it both ways. Mr. and Mrs. Dawson here have seen us on both sides. And look where we're at now! Praise the Lord!"

All the Dawsons sat through this exchange in respectful silence. They were happy for the Knight family, and for their prospects of being more involved with them.

Ardro finally breathed a happy sigh. "Yeah! That's why I'm doin' what I'm doing now. I wanna help more people see both sides. When I'm a detective, I can work at both ends. Right Mr. Dawson?

Mr. Dawson felt a fatherly pride he'd never experienced before. With a warm glow, he nodded. "Yep, Right Ardro! Thanks.

*   *   *

XIV

The Summit

Graduating near the top of his class, Ardro was the first to receive one of Mr. Mongus' scholarships.

His invitations naturally included Helene, Uncle Berty and Miss Tina. He had entrance tickets for all of them, but he reserved one ticket for his Daddy, Ray Knight.

When Ray received the graduation invitation, he was overwhelmed with emotion. It took him a long agonizing time to decide what to do. Once his mind was made up, nothing could stop him. That morning, he drove six hours to get there.

Now that he had arrived, he experienced a multitude of feelings. He sat in his car, and watched parents and friends file into the auditorium. He was not able to spot Helene in the crowd. He finally entered the rear of the brightly lit Hall just as the ceremony began—thankful that the crowded room hid him, and his face. Delight and pride merged with jealousy and sadness.

To him, the Dark Green clad, graduation line seemed endless. They all looked alike to him. He was finally able to pick Ardro's face out of the sea of faces, but since he didn't know what to expect, he anxiously sat through the opening music and speeches of the ceremony. Finally there came the time for giving out the diplomas.

Fascinated, Ray watched the green procession cross the stage, and the joyful reactions of the happy students. The name, Lydia Dawson, didn't mean a thing to him, but as he watched Ardro's face when she received her diploma, he could tell that she was important to him. Through it all, he could feel himself becoming more nervous, as he anxiously waited for Ardro's turn.

Then, when his name was announced, Ardro strode proudly toward the Principal. As Ray watched Mr. Browne put the diploma into Ardro's hand, he was overcome with a profound sadness that he had missed most of Ardro's life. At the same time, he felt the almost aching pride that he was Ardro's father, and that his son had achieved an important goal—one that he had missed. These feelings mixed with the incredible delight that he could be there to witness it all.

During the ceremony, Ray kept a sorrowful eye on a glowing Helene sitting up in the front row. Her proudly smiling brother Berty, was two seats away. As Ray watched her, he felt the loneliness and vacancy of a deep loss. He could only look—from the outside—at the joy of his family; the family he should have helped to this point.

Helene didn't know that Ardro had seen Ray when he entered. She kept wondering what her boy was staring at. She thought he was just nervous, but when he received the diploma, she could see that he was at ease. He grinned the widest smile she had ever seen, and then he winked at her, and yelled. "Love ya, Mom!" As he strutted across the stage, he bowed flamboyantly to the dawsons. When he straightened up, he held the diploma high, and said a loud, "Hey, Dad!"

Helene gasped, and almost fell out of the seat. And Ray cried.

For a long moment, her happiness that Ray was there for Ardro mingled with anger, exasperation, annoyance and a strange, long-forgotten love. "Now, he shows up." She fussed silently. And, in the next breath, "God Bless 'im!" She stood up to try to see him. Then put him out of her mind during the rest of the presentation of diplomas.

The rest of the ceremony, and the vision of Mr. Mongus striding toward the podium interrupted the thoughts that she had after that. She sat back down and closed her eyes in prayer and thanksgiving, as he began to speak. Then she sat in agitation that his speech was taking too long.

Finally, he made the announcement:

"Ladies and Gentlemen! With great pleasure and happiness tonight, I present the first of the scholarships from the Mongus Inc. Community Education Foundation. This one, in the amount of $3,000.00 is awarded to our honor student—and Helene held her breath as he was about to say—, "Mr. Ardro Knight."

"He has been accepted into the Criminal Justice program at Howard University."

The crowd went wild with applause.

Ray used the cover of this jubilant opportunity to disappear. He probably foresaw what was about to happen. His abrupt departure probably saved him from further ecstatic agony. By the time Helene scanned the back rows he was gone.

On his way out, Ray saw and approached a person he was sure was a monitor—either a security officer or a teacher. With tear-filled eyes, he spoke to, and took the man's hand, and gently placed into it an envelope.

He timidly asked, "Would you please, see that My Son, Ardro Knight, gets this letter?"

"Uh, Yes . . . . Yes, sure. I certainly will, . . . Mr. . . . Mr. . . . Knight?" Said the astounded teacher, as he watched Ray rush—as if in a daze—out the door.

Ardro didn't see Ray leave. But, at about that time, he ambled toward Mr. Mongus at the podium.

He felt Mr. Mongus' strong handshake, and tried to return it. He gasped for air, and his grip failed him for a split second. Then, with his face radiant, due to his excitement, and a two-hand vice like grip, he almost yelled, "**Thank you, Mr. Mongus and all of you. I Will Honor this and Make it Good!**"

He turned to face the audience, and waited until they were all quiet. He calmed himself down, and with his face glowing, as he looked at Helene. He quietly said, "Momma, we did it."

The audience roared again, as Helene buried her head in her lap and rocked with emotion.

Haltingly, he then spoke of the loving care of his Principal, the Counselors, all of his teachers and friends—living and dead—who helped him.

Turning to Mr. Browne he said, "Mr. Browne, Can I take minute?"

With Mr. Browne's nod, he resolutely faced the full house, and with a long pensive sigh, started.

"Ladies and Gentlemen, I gotta say something. You all have helped me learn something very important.

In a mixture of pain and exultation, he said, "I nearly turned school loose, and I know I almost made my Momma give up on me. Thank God that didn't happen! But a lotta things happened to me along the way that's still happening to too many of my friends. I am real lucky that some of those hard knocks in my time made me tighten my grip."

"One of those awful bumps in the road made me begin to realize that I CAN do it, if I would just hang on!

And I did—I did hang on, because I was too scared to fall off. I hung on. And now I'm here, because I realized that God, and Momma and I were not going to be beat."

There was stunned silence.

"So," He continued with deep emotion. "I figured out, that if I would stick with whatever I had to do and believe in myself, everything I want for me and Momma could happen."

Then with a pause, and a deep breath, he stressed. "I hope all you guys out there will find this out before its too late. Your journey's different from mine, but if you listen—and really hear—the goodwill all around you, your journey can take you to a good place too."

He stood erect, amid the hearty applause of the crowd.

Then along with an especially loving glance to Liddy, he expressed thanks and gratitude to the Dawsons for pointing him in the career direction he has chosen.

He finished by thanking Mr. Mongus for his eventual recognition of the needs of young people in the community, and for taking the lead in this project.

"At this very minute," He announced. "I am the first of many more. This is one of the most priceless minutes in my lifetime.

As he headed to his seat, he shouted. "Thank **All** of you!"

Helene, bursting with pride and happiness, bounced up out of her seat, and the audience followed, with a rousing standing ovation. She was so overwhelmed that she started singing at the top of her voice, ***"Praise God From Whom All Blessings Flow"*** The whole audience joined in. That was the grand way the program ended.

The happy recessional flowed into the gym. In the midst of all the excitement, Ardro and Helene heard a voice from behind.

"Ardro!"

They looked around, and saw a teacher approaching them.

"Oh, Hello Mr. Gillis." said Helene, smiling.

Mr. Gillis greeted and congratulated them, then soberly said, "Ardro, I have something for you. Here, . . . a man, apparently your father, asked me to give you this letter. He was very wistful, and he left, just a few minutes ago, in a great hurry."

"Thank you, Mr. Gillis."

Mr. Gillis then scurried away, saying "Well anyway, Congratulations. We're all so proud and happy for you."

They looked at the envelope, then at each other, before they claimed a settee in the lobby. Helene held her breath as Ardro unsteadily opened the envelope. Out of it fell two pieces of paper—one a money order for $700.00, and the other a barely legible handwritten note:

My only Son,

You are the only thing I have, that I can feel proud about. I don't feel proud about me, because I can't take no credit for making you the way you are. Use this little bit of money to help you keep on doing good. And . . . be a good Daddy.

Sorry I wasn't around to love you all your life, but I do now.

Love
Ray

* * *